CW01664679

The Worst Self-Help Guru EVER!

The Unconventional Path to Overcoming the Condition of Busyness

Lisa Powney

Author: Lisa Powney @2024
Title: The Worst Self-help Guru Ever!
(The unconventional path to overcoming the condition of busyness.)

ISBN: 978-1-7384171-5-5

Category: Personal Development/Self-help/Health
Publisher: Breakfree Forever Publishing

The Worst Self-Help Guru EVER!

The Unconventional Path to Overcoming the Condition of Busyness

Lisa Powney

Breakfree Forever Publishing

The Worst Self-Help Guru EVER!

Foreword

Embracing Imperfection
The Unconventional Self-Help Journey

In a world filled with polished self-help gurus and glossy success stories, Lisa Powney stands apart as a beacon of raw honesty and authenticity. Through her book, she fearlessly embraces being the worst self-help guru ever, revealing her own missteps, doubts, and struggles to find her way back to herself.

I first met Lisa nearly a year ago and was immediately captivated by her genuine nature. She exuded warmth and kindness, yet beneath her smile, I sensed a longing to reclaim the vibrant spirit she once possessed. Life had thrown its fair share of challenges her way, and the role of caring for her son, the lively and adorable Freddie, had consumed her every waking moment. It was during this period that Lisa lost herself amidst the busyness of daily life and forgotten dreams.

However, fate had other plans. As our paths intertwined professionally, I had the privilege of witnessing Lisa's transformation firsthand. With unwavering determination, she embarked on a powerful journey of self-reflection, rebuilding her confidence piece by piece. It was through her commitment to her framework she created and an unwavering belief in her own worth that she began to shine once again.

This book not only serves as a testament to Lisa's personal growth but also as a work through journal, packed with lots of quirky questions and practical tasks. With each turn of the page, she showers readers with vulnerability, truth and humor, inviting them to walk alongside her as she shares the highs and lows, the triumphs and missteps on her path to a balanced life.

In a society fixated on perfection and quick fixes, Lisa breaks the mold by emphasising the importance of self-acceptance and self-compassion.

She reminds us that it is okay to stumble, to be the least likely person to guide others in their personal journeys because sometimes, it is our own struggles that equip us with the most profound insights and wisdom.

As the pages unfold, you will witness Lisa's metamorphosis from a lost soul to a confident woman who has reconnected with her true essence. Along the way, she uncovers the transformative power of self-love, highlighting its role as the cornerstone of her own personal growth.

Dear reader, prepare to embark on an unconventional yet profoundly rewarding journey. Lisa Powney's honest and relatable narrative will inspire you to embrace imperfection, to celebrate your quirks, and to love yourself unconditionally. Through her story, you will find solace, courage, and, most importantly, the guidance to prioritise your own well-being to prevent burnout.

So, open your heart and mind, and let Lisa's words guide you on a path to a better well being one that celebrates the beauty in imperfection and the resilience of the human spirit.

Remember, it is through embracing our own journey, warts and all, that we find the strength to become the best versions of ourselves.

Well done Lisa.

Jane Leonard
Former England and Army Rugby Player
World Record Holder

Dedicated to my mum and sisters near and far

Lessons learnt from our lovely mum.

Mum, if we had another chance,
to see you for a day.
We'd let you know how much your'e loved,
and what we learned along the way...

Remember to be always kind,
regardless of what you've got.
Because even if it's nothing
Your time will mean a lot.

When naming all your children, (and your dog)
make sure you're not befuddled.
Don't name them all with the letter L
It will lead you to be muddled.

Always have great values,
teach your children right from wrong.
Have markers for their pathways,
that will last their whole life long.

If your life is getting you down,
and you are finding it hard to cope.
Remember those worse off than you,
and watch Jeremy Kyle for some hope.

When your children make a choice,
don't be the judge or jury.
It doesn't matter if you agree or not,
They should never feel your fury.

If you need some cheering up,
because positive thoughts are few.
Get your hair done, and your nails,
and buy some ornaments too!

When it comes to living life,
much of it is tough,
Don't give up, be a fighter,
you're made of sterner stuff.

If you have some money to spare,
and you feel a little flush.
Get yourself on QVC,
and buy jewellery that is plush.

Family is a special gift,
That shouldn't be overlooked.
Work together, be there
grow love that can't be shook.

Mum
We know we were your reason,
we are your legacy.
We hope you know how much you're loved
you will always be part of us three.

Written by Lisa Powney – Eulogy for my mums funeral

I love you mum, I love you girls, you are my inspiration and reason... always X
I love you Freddie with all my heart, You are my world x

Contents

Preface

Its Sunday morning, and my 3-year-old son and I are cuddling on the sofa, enjoying a Disney favourite, Moana. I'm smiling ear to ear as I listen to him singing the lines of "You're Welcome" - he knows every word! And then the phone rings...

It's my youngest sister: she unusually tells me she is dialling in my middle sister, and we end up on a group call. 'Mum has had a fall,' she says 'Denise her next-door neighbour, called. She says she's ok and just having a cup of tea, but wanted to let us know. I'm going over now. Unusually, all 3 of us decide to pop over to see how mum is doing.

I don't rush; instead I call my son's dad, and unusually, he decides to come too, just in case I need to anything for my mum. "Thoughtful,' I think but probably not needed. I let him, though.

In the car, my son is singing along to another of his favourite songs. "Hey, sweetheart, Auntie is calling...' 'Hi Lou! The panic in her voice makes my stomach turn over. 'Lisa, I'm here, and it's really bad. Please get here soon...'My heart beats so fast, and hot tears start to come down my cheeks... I'm panicking. 'Mummy, what's the matter with Nannie? I don't like it.' Kids sense EVERYTHING. 'Nothing, sweetheart, it will be okay...' I try my utmost to reassure when, inside, every part of me feels bad."

The phone rings again; this time it's my middle sister. 'Whatever you do, don't bring Freddie out of the car, okay!' Bad turns to gravely serious in just those few words. As I turn the corner, the paramedics are carrying my mum into the ambulance. She's strapped in and only in her nightdress. Freddie's dad sees it too from his own car and quickly takes Freddie. I run to the ambulance, and the faces of my two sisters will be etched in my mind forever. I'm the eldest, so I take on this role and tell them I will go with mum to the hospital. My sisters are both nurses, and they know I'm not good with medical emergencies, but they let me do this because they know right now I need to do this, for mum, for me, for them. They circle the ambulance feeling lost. We are blue-lighted to the hospital, and I pretend I'm calm... I'm clearly not! As the very kind paramedic tells my mum that she is doing better than me. In my head, I'm thinking, it's a stroke, people recover from strokes, she will be ok, right?

I look at her, she has blood running from her nose and her body is jolting. She is making the most awful noise from her throat, and the paramedic is trying to clear it. She is clearly unconscious, so I wiggle and squeeze her bare feet, willing her on to get better, to hear me, to know I'm with her... she always hated her feet.

She is rushed straight into A & E, the bed is weighed with my mum on it, and she is rushed to the critical bay, I just follow in a daze, on my own wondering what's going to happen. Nobody tells me what to do, so I sit outside the bay she's in and they draw a curtain around her. I hear them hooking her up to machines, and they joke about this being the start of the shift and something else... I am angry because I just want them to focus on her and nobody is telling me anything... until they did!

"Hello, I'm the registrar looking after your mother," I look up, his accent is German, I think. He is a tall man with strong features and to me at this moment shows little warmth. "We have had the results of her brain scan, and she has had a significant bleed on the brain. Unfortunately, there is nothing we can do." This is a real Eastenders Doof Doof Doof moment... and it felt unreal. What? How? I try to keep composed, but I'm crumbling, "what happens now?" I'm sorry, but you just have to wait for your mum to die. I didn't know how to do that, my sisters and I didn't know how to do that. Nothing and nobody can prepare you for that, but we did, and just like that, life was never the same again.

So why am I opening up with this sad story? In the days and weeks that followed that fateful day, I relived every moment in finite detail over and over again, and then it became more chilling. Not only did I relive these desperately sad moments, but memories that I had seemingly locked away for years started to come back. One memory, in particular, haunted me, and maybe that's something I share later with you.

During this time, I was fortunate enough to meet a wonderful counselor, a beautiful soul who helped me wake up to all sorts of things I had never addressed before. I came to see that I had been living a pattern of insignificance to keep me safe, and that my mum had done the same, and my past memories were founded in this too. Weirdly, although I sobbed uncontrollably at times and felt desperately sad as the layers were peeled back, I felt this fearless optimism that this awareness would redefine me in the most positive way. I didn't know how or why, I just knew.I have been writing this book for a while now, and I kept getting stuck... I have such a passion for helping people thrive, be the best they can be, but I hold back on my ideas and being seen. I was asked a poignant question: "When you are on the cusp of being successful, what is it that stops you from progressing? What does this 'Success' look like for you?"

"I hold back because I am disappointed with where I have gotten to now in my late 40s. I'm constantly striving for the next thing, but when asked, I actually can't articulate for myself what I really want. It literally petrifies me! I'm a single mom always 'being busy,' in the most unsustainable financial position I have ever been, downsizing on everything, in a career I wouldn't necessarily choose... and a body I refuse to recognize anymore... and I want to talk to people about their well-being and personal success. My god, I'm the worst self-help guru ever! And I laugh, and she laughs, and says, 'But I think maybe that's what real people want to hear about.' And hence the title of this book...

Having come quite a long way, I'm still not there, but the positive feeling hasn't diminished. So for those of you out there who want a hand to hold, to feel that someone is trying and failing and then learning just like you, but with a positive hope that together we have got each other's back and we can move forward, and maybe have a laugh about it along the way. If this is you, then come with me on this journey and let's see where it takes us both!...

6th June 2021, the day my life changed forever...

"It's good to laugh at yourself, especially when you trip over nothing as I often do!"

— LISA POWNEY

Introduction

Dear amazing person who decided to give this book a go...

Welcome to a one-of-a-kind adventure! And when I say unique, I truly mean it because as I write these words, I have no idea where this journey will lead us. However, I have hope that this will be a place of self-reflection, self-awareness, and perhaps even some self-improvement. But let's be honest, as you can tell from the title, I'm not making any promises! So, be prepared to put in some effort alongside me!

As we delve into the upcoming chapters, I invite you to embark on your own personal mission of navigating this fast-paced world while discovering more about yourself. But before we proceed any further, let's make an important agreement... Together, we may uncover some uncomfortable truths, and that's perfectly okay. I will be right here with you every step of the way. However, I ask that we learn and grow together without taking ourselves too seriously.

For those who know me, I have a reputation for stumbling over absolutely nothing. It's a talent I've had forever, much to the amusement of my friends and family. No matter how careful I am or how focused I try to be, I somehow find a way to trip or lose my balance. And I'm not talking about a simple stumble; I'm talking about epic faceplants accompanied by flailing arms and embarrassed laughter. It's as if gravity has a personal vendetta against me, and I'm its favourite target. My missteps have become legendary among my loved ones, and they never miss an opportunity to remind me of my not-so-graceful nature.

I've tried everything to improve my balance and coordination. From yoga classes to tai chi, and even attempting to walk with a book on my head like they do in those old movies. But no matter how hard I try, I always end up on the ground, much to the delight of anyone lucky enough to witness my clumsiness. Despite the constant embarrassment, I've learned to embrace my talent for falling over nothing. It has become a defining characteristic of mine, and I've come to realise that it's alright to be a little unsteady on my feet. After all, life is full of unexpected obstacles, both literal and metaphorical, and being able to laugh at myself when I stumble is a valuable skill.

So, the next time you see me take a tumble for no apparent reason, don't worry. I'm probably not hurt, just practicing my signature move. And who knows, maybe one day I'll perfect the art of falling over nothing and turn it into a dazzling dance routine. But until then, I'll continue to embrace my talent and provide endless entertainment for those around me.

Now, where are we headed with all of this?...Do you agree that life can often feel like a whirlwind of expectations, deadlines, and constant demands, leaving us with little time for reflection and personal growth? I understand because I live it too. So, yes, I hear you! This is where I want this journal to come to our aid. My intention for this book is to be your companion, a place where you can hold space for your thoughts, ideas, smiles, and aspirations amidst the chaos of everyday life. Intrigued? I certainly hope so...

Throughout the upcoming chapters, you will come across thought-provoking prompts, real stories, guided reflections, and practical exercises. I want this book to be more than just reading; it's about taking action towards a more positive life and well-being. The key to this is to take action without placing too many expectations on ourselves. If it works, great! If not, let's fail fast, learn, and move on to the next action.

"But I have no time!" you might say.

Ha ha! Exactly! I see you!

The intention of this journal is to change that, but it will require setting aside time to create more time. I know, it sounds counter-intuitive, but bear with me. At the end of the first chapter, I will ask you to make a decision for yourself. Do you want to continue this personal mission of change with me? And if so, are you willing to give it the dedication it deserves? I'm thrilled that you've stayed with me thus far. Thank you! Let's be accountability partners, sounding boards for each other, and guides. Let's embrace whatever challenges this journal throws at us, and who knows, by the end, it might just change our lives forever! Fingers crossed!

Now, what else do you need to know? Throughout this journal, I want us to assume a few constants...

Constant 1: You have permission and the right to not take yourself too seriously. (Sense of humour)

Constant 2: You have permission and the right to be kind to yourself throughout this.

Constant 3: You have permission and the right to be brave and step forward with courage.

Now over to you...

"Some days I'm amazing, some days I leave my phone in the fridge, I'm only human after all"

— LISA POWNEY

1

Only H.U.M.A.N

Have you ever heard the saying "You're a human being, NOT a human doing?" Isn't it interesting that most of us spend time doing rather than being?

A little boy of 6 years old runs up the stairs after school. "Mummy, can I tell you something? Can I tell you what happened at school?" The excitement she feels when she sees her mum is immense and her smile lights up the room.

"I'm just on a call, darling. I will be 10 minutes, okay?" "Mummy, how long is 10 minutes? It's not long, go and get yourself a biscuit and I will be with you soon." "Mummy, I'm back! Can I tell you something now? Oh, you are not listening to me!" "Sweetheart, I haven't finished yet, I won't be too long. Can you go and play with something?" "What shall I play?" "Ok, ok, excuse me everyone, I will be right back."

"I tell you what, you know you like jigsaws. Well, you see this picture here of the world in this magazine. If I tear it into small pieces, do you think you could put it back together again for me?" 10 minutes later, he is at the door. "Mummy, Mummy, I have finished it," and holds up the picture of the world with cello tape all over it. "Oh, my, how on earth did you do that?" "It's dead easy, Mummy, because on the other side there is a picture of a HUMAN, and when I put the HUMAN back together, the world just fell into place."

Isn't it a shame that the world gets so busy it takes a child to highlight what's missing?

YOU MIGHT BE THINKING, why is IT important TO TALK ABOUT MAKING THE WORLD A BETTER PLACE? And why this story?

Do you sometimes feel you are on life's carousel, and you can't get off? That you never get the chance to pause or even catch your breath to reflect, to stop and enjoy the moment?

YES! Well, I call this 'go go go' mentality the condition of busyness, and I purposefully call it a 'condition' because its definition is a state of being. And when I say busyness, I don't mean just any kind. I mean the type where you are constantly striving to meet the expectations of others and you of them... it's exhausting!

Johns Hopkins researchers cite this condition as pervasive, unavoidable, and it's damaging our lives, both mentally and physically. And more gravely, it's impacting our ability to have healthy relationships.

EXPECTATION - What a loaded word. It always feels one way... because if it was two-way, then we would call it an AGREEMENT - Hold that thought!

NOW, YOU MIGHT BE THINKING... THIS RESONATES WITH ME AND I DON'T LIKE IT.

FIRSTLY, know it's not your fault, and KNOW you can change it. ALL YOU have to DO IS choose to do something about it. Sounds easy, eh!

So, you might be wondering why I am so passionate about the condition of busyness? Ok, let me take you back to July 2020. It's the third hottest day of the year so far, and the sun is shining into my very plush office. You know the type I'm talking about... the ones with a luxurious chaise longue? I mean, a single bed and plenty of storage... I mean, wardrobes in the background! Yes, it's the early days of lockdown, and I'm on a virtual video call with one of my clients, let's call him Simon. Simon is in his 40s, slim, an avid cyclist, and his hair is starting to grow long and tickle his eyebrows because, of course, no hairdressers are open!

So, you know I came to you because I was feeling stuck in my career, and my "Why," well since then I think I have had a real lightbulb moment...

Oh yeah, what's that then, Simon? I finally realised after our last chat that maybe I am striving for the wrong career aspiration. That the promotion is not really what I want in my life right now. It was just something I felt I ought to chase after for my family... All this pressure to prove myself is making me so unhappy. I'm stressed and overwhelmed, and I'm taking it out at home. The whole reason I'm doing this for is my family... However, I'm burning out at work and then coming home and upsetting them.

Have you ever had a time when you knew a change was needed yet you didn't know where to start?... That's exactly what happened with Simon, and I started to work in a different direction with him, first making a plan about the positive change he wanted to see in his business life.

So let's see what happened a month later. My roots are clearly showing, and now you can hardly see Simon's eyes, and I'm back in my plush office on a virtual call with Simon.

"How are you doing, Simon, since we last spoke?"

"Yes things are much better personally, I have noticed a difference in how I'm feeling."

"Good Simon, how are things at home with you and your wife?"

"So here's an interesting thing, Lisa (Interestingly, I notice he is playing with his wedding ring and wonder what that is all about). I'm now going home, and I feel calmer, but the minute I come through the door, she's like taking a step away from me, and I almost feel like I have put her on eggshells because she is so used to me firing off. I'm not doing it as much anymore, but she's still reacting in that way, and the kids seem distant too. I really don't know what else to do."

"Oh, right, that's interesting, Simon. How long has it been going on like this?"

"I'm not sure how long. Maybe I have been too busy to notice, but I definitely see it and feel it now."

"Simon, that's okay. Let's focus on this and see where we can get to."

So after he shared with me, I went away and started to look at a different aspect with this client. I started to look at things from a whole life perspective. So here we are again, back on our virtual call 2 weeks later... but this time he looks different somehow. His hair is cut, he has had a shave, and somehow just looks more in control.

He's beaming, and the first thing he tells me is that he now feels frigging human again. "I did everything you said and slowly things have started to change. I realized that it was a lot to do with me, my stuff, and my anger. Everyone at home was on eggshells with everything I did, and now we are all talking and working it all out together."

"That's such great news, Simon." "Yes, it is, and I'm grateful to you for listening. I have never talked about this stuff with anybody before, and it's the kick up the arse I needed."

"You should do more of this with people. I don't think I will be the only person who's experiencing what I experienced." Anticipating expectations and meeting needs is ingrained in me, and quite frankly, these conversations really resonated with me and made me think about my own condition of busyness. I started looking for more tools and resources. And so, I guess there was where the H.U.M.A.N Bounce Back Recovery program began.

I'd love to share that it was all easy and within weeks I'd turned into a transformational wizard...but as we all know life doesn't work that easily- There were moments of doubt.

I thought about what my colleagues might say. "Do you think people want to talk about their personal life in business?... I don't think so!"

I thought friends and family may say, "Who do you think you are, some kind of business Oprah Winfrey? Nah!"

Inside my inner voice was shouting. The condition of busyness, isn't that just a fad! And then I was reminded of the story I shared with you earlier...

I realised, however, we are all only human, and expectations at work and home are intrinsically linked...

So you might be wondering why I am so passionate about this. Well, you know the playing of the wedding ring, where I knew something was wrong? You see, that level of noticing came about because of my role within my family from the age of 7 – 14. I was to be on watch. You see, most days, you would find me in the front bedroom window from around 5.30pm, looking down, waiting to see what mood my father was in when he got home. Did he look red-faced? Was he huffing and puffing? Did he look angry? Would he be slamming the van door shut? Because you see, if that was what he was like, then we, my two younger sisters, my mum, and I, all had to take our positions or hide. And that happened until I was 14.

But when I was 14, things became so terrifying. We had to escape from our family home, and I use that word on purpose because that's what it was. Being highly attuned to others' expectations came from living with a father who was violently abusive, a father who was under pressure, who overworked in a job he hated, and wasn't living the dream he wanted to. He came home every day and took it out on us in the worst possible way. I NEVER want any child to witness what I witnessed and lose their childhood, and I also don't want any parent to be like that again or miss out on their kids.

I would love to say that it was only paper that was torn into pieces, but it wasn't. It was people, and they are much harder to put back together. I haven't seen my father for 34 years. He missed out on the growing up of three girls and has never seen his beautiful grandchildren. Isn't it a shame that he couldn't be the complete man and not only make a difference to his own life but the next two generations that came after him?

So now you know why I am so passionate about this. Let's talk about YOU and see how YOU could become more of the human you are meant to be too.

Now, I'd love to say I have cracked it and I'm there as the "sorted human I'm meant to be," but GOD NO, I'm still working on it. What I am good at, though, is reflecting on and appreciating my learning from all my many misadventures... and if you can do that, then you can experience wisdom and growth beyond any course or book. That's what being only HUMAN really means. So if you want to join me in learning from my 'not what to do' and reflecting on your own, then jump in and let's see what happens.

Through learning from what not to do, I have come to realize that there are probably just five steps that you need in order to be able to have balance in your life. Now, these five steps interestingly do spell the word **Human.**

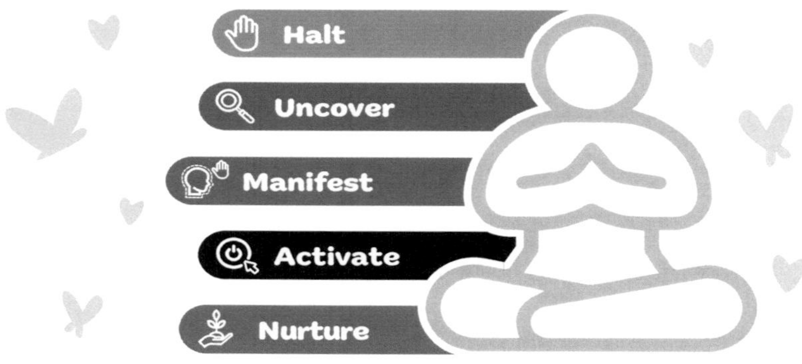

Only H.U.M.A.N Bounceback Recovery Programme.

Are you someone who thrives on non-stop action and endless to-do lists, never needing time to pause? Make space for yourself, just in case you might let the real world come in? For a long time, and sometimes still, this was me too! Who needs time to really take in how unhappy you might be, or how unfulfilled or lost? It's much better to say yes to everyone else, meet their needs, and leave yourself exhausted at the end of each day. You have little option other than to fall into bed and try to catch some sleep. Or is it??

For those of you who are curious about a different kind of life, who are tempted to see what being the human they are meant to be could look like, you may want to try the first step of **HALT**. So what do I mean by that?

Well, many of my clients, when they don't halt, find that their diaries manage them. They take on too much, feel overworked, and ultimately, their resilience and well-being are impacted. However, when my clients allow themselves to halt, they are able to pause and make the space they need to review where they truly are. In this stage, they find a way to stop managing others and start managing themselves better.

Ok, so I have had a bit of "me time," you might say. Is that all it takes? And as a well-known supermarket says, "every little helps." But it's been years living in this way. It's habitual, and in many ways, there is no concept of what could be different. Besides, isn't it better to put others first, just react to life, and let it control you? I'm sure that's what trusting the universe is all about. Or is it???

For those with a itsy bitsy bit of belief that maybe life could be different, then you may want to move to the next step, which is **UNCOVER.**

In this step, my clients see the need to take a fresh look at themselves and what might be driving their level of busyness. I don't know about you, but sometimes I wear my busyness as a badge of honour. If I am not super busy, then I must need to care more about my job, my family, my home, my friends, my neighbours, even! Have you ever wondered what might be behind this need to fill our time? What might you be avoiding or turning away from instead?

So you have put your new perspective glasses on, great. But then you still feel compelled to say "Yes" to meeting everyone else's expectations, putting their needs before your own. Believe me, I have been there. Isn't the way to get ahead to be the ultimate people pleaser? Or is it??

If there's even a slight adverse reaction to being a people pleaser, then, like many of my clients, you may want to move to the next step: **MANIFEST**. So what do I mean by "Manifest"? Your head may switch straight to, "Oh, here we go... spiritual woo woo." Yes and no, there's a lot to be said for the power of the universe; however, in this instance, I'm talking about manifesting in the more practical sense "to make clear or evident." In this step, my clients spend the time to manifest their new boundaries, and in the words of the great philosophers, the Spice Girls, focus in on what they really, really want... zig a zig ahh, and just as importantly, what they don't want.

Let's be honest, there is one small word out there when used well can change your life, but many struggle to say it, embody it, and handle it in the right way...

So, you might be thinking, "Come on Lisa... what's the word?" Well, it's the opposite of "yes"; the word is "no" (and I mean the very small version of that word, N-O).

OK, let's just have a recap, just for those who are considering the possibility of discovering their HUMAN inside...

First, you need to halt, to pause and make space to understand where you are. Then, you uncover where you might need some help, and then you put into practice manifest for what you want and what you don't want going forward. So now you have two options:

Option 1 - This one I have chosen many, many times before – The **F*ALL** Option, I mean the "do F* all with it" option. Appreciate that you started the process and put some effort in, but jump out when it gets too close to actually taking real action.

Or

Option 2 - You could give yourself a kick up the arse and finally get into action in a structured and productive way and give it **ALL** option. I like to call this the **ACTIVATE** option or step.

Have you ever had a time when you put in loads of effort into making a change, things were different for a while and you were motivated, and then your "other voice" kicked in and said, "Go on, it won't do you any harm to fall back into your own ways... you can always jump back in on your 'New way' once you're done?" You don't want this new way to become a habit that sticks, right? Or do you??

For those of you out there that think maybe it's a time for out with the old and in with the new, then my final step is all about **NURTURE**, nurturing the changes you have committed to for the long term, understanding what you need to do to make this change stick and allow this new way of being human to become your new reality.

These five steps - Halt, Uncover, Manifest, Activate, and Nurture - as you can see all spell the word HUMAN.

So let's go back to the first step - **HALT**. If this is something you fancy having a go at, you might be thinking, "How do you do that then?" To help my clients understand the power of HALT, I developed the Balanced Life Blueprint. It is a four-step process that helps people to get into the right place and frame of mind, to have a deep dive look at what's really going on for them because if they don't stop the hamster wheel, then nothing will change.

The second step is **UNCOVER**, focusing on how to get to the core of what has been driving your condition of busyness. For this, I have developed the Personal Assessment Principles. So here, we will work together through an 8-step process to uncover what's important to you, where you are doing things brilliantly, where you can excel even more, and where you may need some attention and help. Because if you don't know what you don't know – some may call these blind spots – you won't know what to do instead.

Once you uncover the root of the matter, you can move to **Manifest** where you will develop your confidence to turn YES into a No or Not now when that's the right thing for you. Using my Calm Cadence Creator, it will help YOU understand how to use the word 'NO' for your benefit, as well as ways to take charge of what you really want. Without this, clients struggle to stop doing things that don't serve them, that take energy away and don't give anything back.

Then it's **Activate**, If you choose to do nothing, the process is clear: just abandon all previous gains and let the progress disappear. For those who choose to kick themselves into action, I have developed the 90-day positive performance plan. In 90 days, you can identify, with a clear head, those laser-focused actions that will really make a difference and commit to them for positive change. Those who do can be confident that whatever they put their time into going forward will be important and add value. Those who don't will have done some great thinking, and that might be enough!

Finally, it's **Nurture**. For this, I have developed the simple Measurable Maps Method to keep you in action on the right things at the right time, allowing for peak performance and happiness at work, and most importantly, outside of work. For those of you who want to bail at the first sign of things becoming a habit, then make your excuses as to why this wasn't the right change for you and carry on with life as you know it. I have done so for a long time, so I get it!

For those of you who want help to be the human that you really are, I call this system the 'Only H.U.M.A.N Bounce Back Recovery Program', helping you to not only bounce back from moments of doubt and negative thoughts, but also bounce back into being the best human you can be. In this book, I will introduce you to each of these steps and some of the strategies that support them. I will hold your hand through each step, and at the end of each chapter, there will be exercises and questions for you to answer. Give yourself some time to do this and enjoy the process.

I'm looking forward to holding space for you over the coming chapters. So, as I said, I must ask: do you still want to continue this personal mission of change with me? And if so, are you willing to give it the dedication it deserves? Yes... Let's go!

"Honestly now I'm so busy, I'm too busy to tell people how busy I am"

— LISA POWNEY

2

Halt

I'm certain that you're familiar with the saying "Pause to go faster!" It's a mantra often preached by self-help gurus, and I have personally shared this advice countless times, emphasizing the benefits of slowing down to achieve more. In theory, it makes perfect sense. So, why is it incredibly challenging to put into practice?

Now, let me take you back to the end of the summer term when I was in my final year of primary school. I knew that today was the day my school report would be sent home. Having experienced this moment for several years, I was familiar with the routine, yet the fear of my grades still gripped me. I desperately hoped that this time I would have straight A's, but deep down, I knew it was unlikely. School was an average game for me, and I had to exert immense effort to keep up. The thought of not meeting expectations weighed heavily on me.

As I stood at the school gates, my mum appeared. "Hello, are you alright?" she asked. "Yes, Mum, I'm alright. I have the school report," I replied. She immediately suggested stopping at the park on our way home so we could change my grades before my father arrived. She hadn't seen my report yet, but she already anticipated that it wouldn't be good enough.

When I finally showed her the report, it revealed four C's, a few C+'s, a B, and an A (thankfully). My mum quickly skimmed over the comments and fixated on the C's, determined to transform them into A's and even an A+ (which didn't even exist). To me, it seemed painfully obvious every year, but she believed that these altered grades would be enough to convince my father that I had achieved straight A's. Have you ever experienced a situation where you did your absolute best, but it still fell short of the mark?

My mum's intention was not to hurt my feelings; rather, she wanted to shield me from disappointment and make me more lovable through academic achievement. My father placed immense value on being intellectually gifted, and if you didn't meet that standard, you were deemed unworthy of love...

Many people are taught at a young age that they are more lovable when they achieve. These children can turn into workaholic adults who have difficulty knowing their own worth and accepting unconditional love. I became one of these adults with an additional critical flaw: I crave unconditional love to define my self-worth... It's been an interesting journey!

I'm an all-or-nothing kind of girl. As far back as I can remember, I have used busyness as a form of escapism. It has served to dull down my emotions, and those times that I have slowed down have brought more fear than I ever could have imagined...I worked in the head office of a bank, running a team of 20. It was the first time in my life that I had a job I sought after, got, and loved. As I write this for the first time, I'm making the connection between a real desire for a career and truly loving what I do. Every other job I have had, I have somehow fallen into. It has either been suggested to me, given to me, or I have felt I should go for it. I have mostly gone with it, except for two occasions where some overwhelming feeling took over and I opted out. But, more on this later... now, getting back to the job I loved.

It's 7:30 am and I'm parking in the center of the city, having left the house at 6:30 am as I usually do. I'm not naturally an early bird, so I have to get up extra early to be anywhere near awake for my drive into the city. I walk out of the car park and towards the office. I notice a man coming towards me. He's tall and blonde. As he moves nearer, I think to myself, "he's nice, he looks like Michael Buble." He smiles at me and nods, and I smile back and think nothing of it. I continue to the office entrance. Inside, I make my usual first pit stop at Starbucks. I still get a buzz from having our own Starbucks inside the building. It makes me feel that I work somewhere important, for some reason (weird, maybe that's why I have a massive coffee habit). Up the stairs to the 4th floor and in through the double doors, I'm one of the first to arrive. I will work at my desk and be ready to welcome my team, then I will have back-to-back meetings for most of the day. There's a good deal of fire-fighting that I can choose to get involved in, and I thrive off putting on my Wonder Woman pants and fixing things for others. This all means that at 5 pm, when most people are thinking of leaving, I'm just getting to the stuff that only I can do.

I have been working on a report for at least an hour and a half when Janet and Paul walk in. Janet is in her late 50s, slim, smiley with kind eyes. She keeps her white hair in a lovely bun and wears a burgundy overall. She carries a bucket of cleaning materials, and Paul, her husband, also in his late 50s, has a lean and wiry frame reflecting his active and physically demanding job. His weathered face shows the signs of a life spent working outdoors. Paul's hair is thinning and greying, and he keeps it neatly combed. They make a beeline for me, as they do most nights, but today they smile, albeit with a tinge of sadness, and they are carrying a Warren James gift bag and card. Unusually, they sit on either side of me, and Janet passes me the bag and card. "We just want to say thank you for being lovely with us and taking the time to speak to us. We are so gutted that you are leaving and wanted to get you something." If you hadn't guessed, Janet and Paul are the cleaners at the bank, and for a good while now, they have chatted with me most nights, as the last person leaving the floor.

We have come to know each other well, I say well, but… I know about their home and family, and they know I'm a busy at work kind of person, I'm not one for giving too much away! But 2 months ago, on the same day I won "Leader of the Year," I was told I am being made redundant if

I don't want other roles on offer, as my dream job has disappeared from the structure. I take the redundancy with a heavy heart, and today is my last day. What they don't know is that in recent times, my attempts to have a baby after 6 years have now closed its doors. My marriage is on its last legs, and my house will be sold, leaving me with very little to show for the 20 years I have been with my husband. I'm 36, and nobody at work had a clue that this was going on. Being busy has become my sanctuary, a place where I can avoid dealing with anything... That's my way because slowing down would be much harder. It would mean facing tough questions in my life now, bringing to the surface the emotional pain and forcing me to think about what is the meaning of life now? Have I wasted all that time? Will the grass be greener on the other side? Who wants to face into that... Not me!

After some long hugs, Janet and Paul continue on with their cleaning and hear Janet say to Paul, "I can't wait to see Michael Buble in concert tomorrow. He's playing tonight as well, isn't he?" Blinking heck! It was him, I think. If only I had known... and I fantasise about what I would have done if I had 😊. I pack my bag for the last time, log off, and walk towards the lift, and as loud as you like, I hear Janet shout behind me, "You go and show them, Lisa, what they have lost. Go and be your brilliant self!" I'm touched beyond words...

With a new job in hand and a search for a new home, I continue this cycle of busyness and avoid any moments of pause by filling it with spontaneous nights out or weekends away. This pattern continues until I'm forced to stop.

Learning to Halt

This year is my son's second year at primary school, and on Mondays, we have gotten into a lovely routine. I pick him up from school, and together we go to the library to read and choose books. He loves it, and I'm so pleased. He eats books for breakfast! Before this started, I hadn't been in a library for a long time, and as I entered for the first time again, an overwhelming sense of calm came over me, and I found myself smiling from ear to ear. Time passed so quickly, and once we had chosen the books, we followed it up with a coffee and a treat... gorgeous!

Growing up in a volatile environment, it was rare to find a time of calm except at school. And now, as I sat thinking about the library, I remembered being taken to the local library as a child and feeling that sense of safety burying my head in a book, and having the chance to take them home and lose myself in them.

Every child needs a safe place to fall - a place where he or she can explore things without worrying about failure and judgment. A library is one of those places. - Bill Harley

So why am I telling you about this? This small routine has become one of my tools in the first part of my framework, Halt. I have come to learn that the library or a bookshop has a very calming and healing effect on me. The feel of a book in my hand, or even a few words from a page that feels relevant, can bring a level of peace that nothing else quite compares to.

Okay, I think it's time to get into this. What do we mean by **Halt**?

Have you ever experienced a moment when you sensed you were teetering on a metaphorical cliff edge? Where one more thing, trigger, or responsibility was likely to push you over the edge, but you carried on anyway?

It's December 2021, and as mentioned earlier, my mum had passed away. It had been a tough few months and to be honest, I had never felt loss like it. It hurt beyond anything I had experienced before, and so many questions and emotions filled my head that it was hard to think about much else. Usually, in tough times, I have been able to use the focus of work as a distraction, but this time it didn't seem to be having the same impact. Everything felt insignificant, especially the negatives. I mean, nobody died, except my mum, that is! However, I failed to pause and take in where I was at. I pushed on regardless and kept myself exceptionally busy.

During this time, I led running a major client event. I put the hours in, had all the meetings, knew the drill, but at the same time, I wasn't feeling it. I was anxious, and because of this, I missed a few things. I sensed that they could go wrong but failed to act on it. Overall, the event still went well, but enough didn't hit the mark that a feedback review session was called for. I planned it with a level of dread, and as the feedback came flooding in, I was overcome by shame. Tears flooded my eyes, and my fight/flight response kicked in big time. I couldn't wait to get off the call, and I knew immediately that something serious had broken within me, and there was no way I could face work again anytime soon. This was the first time I took time off for stress, and even knowing this pushed me further down that rabbit hole. I continued to spiral for some time, putting self-care at the bottom of my list. My mind and body suffered as I piled on the weight and spent very little time outside the house. Does any of this resonate with you?

In recent times, I recognize the signs much earlier and take some steps to Halt. I have come to realize that focusing on myself is so important. I need to fill my cup before I can be anything for others.

"**Halt**" essentially means recognising the need to pause, reassess, and make intentional changes to prevent burnout from escalating. It's an acknowledgment that continuing on the current path may have detrimental effects on one's health and overall well-being. Within my program, I have created The Balanced Life Blueprint to help you with this. It's a 4-step process, and taking these steps can contribute to a healthier work-life balance and promote long-term resilience.

The Balanced Life Blueprint

Creating a balanced life blueprint involves identifying your priorities and finding ways to allocate time, energy, and resources to each aspect of your life. Remember, balance looks different for everyone, and it may take some trial and error to find what works best for you. Be kind to yourself throughout the process and celebrate small successes along the way. Here are some steps to help you create your own balanced life blueprint:

Halt

Balanced Life Blueprint
Review - where you are right now, hold up a mirror and take stock of how you currently spend your time and energy. Identify any imbalances or areas where you are neglecting your priorities. This could involve tracking your daily activities for a week or two to gain a better understanding of how you currently allocate your resources.
Remove - clutter and simplify: Streamline your physical and digital spaces to reduce unnecessary distractions and clutter. This will create a more peaceful environment and make it easier to focus on what truly matters.
Reset - your mindset. A balanced life involves adopting a holistic approach that prioritises various aspects of life equally. Strive for balance in all areas of life, including work, relationships, health, hobbies, and personal growth. Avoid neglecting any aspect and allocate time and energy accordingly to maintain equilibrium.
Resources - as a support system. Surround yourself with supportive and positive people who encourage your quest for balance. Seek advice, guidance, and inspiration from mentors, friends, or family members who share similar values and goals. Build a toolkit of resources that you know take you to being present: Practice mindfulness and focus on being fully present in the moment. Avoid dwelling on the past or worrying excessively about the future. This allows you to fully engage in activities and relationships, enhancing your overall sense of balance.

Step 1: Review

Keep a diary of everything you do from waking up to going to sleep, including the timings, for a week. Categorise your activities as follows:

1. **Work/Career**: Record the amount of time you spend on work-related tasks, including commuting, attending meetings, and completing assignments.
2. **Personal Development**: Dedicate a section to the time you spend on learning new skills, such as reading books, attending workshops, or taking online courses.
3. **Physical Health**: Allocate time for exercise, meal preparation, and taking care of your overall physical well-being.
4. **Mental Health**: Note the time you spend on activities that promote mental well-being, such as meditation, journaling, or therapy.
5. **Relationships**: Keep track of the time you spend with family, friends, and loved ones, and assess the quality of these interactions.
6. **Hobbies and Interests**: Dedicate a section to the time you spend on activities you enjoy, such as playing a musical instrument, painting, or practicing a sport.
7. **Leisure and Entertainment**: Record the time you spend on leisure activities like watching TV, browsing social media, or playing video games.
8. **Household Chores**: Allocate time for daily chores, cleaning, grocery shopping, and other household responsibilities.
9. **Sleep**: Note the time you allocate for sleep and evaluate if it is sufficient for your overall well-being.
10. **Other**: Include any additional categories that may be relevant to your specific lifestyle, such as volunteering, community involvement, or personal projects

Your Schedule

Week Date:

Category	Monday	Tuesday	Wednesday	Thursday	Friday	Saturday	Sunday
Work/Career	Hrs Activity	Hrs Activity	Hrs Activity	Hrs Activity	Hrs Activity	Hrs Activity	Hrs Activity
Personal Development	Hrs Activity	Hrs Activity	Hrs Activity	Hrs Activity	Hrs Activity	Hrs Activity	Hrs Activity
Physical Health	Hrs Activity	Hrs Activity	Hrs Activity	Hrs Activity	Hrs Activity	Hrs Activity	Hrs Activity

Category	Monday	Tuesday	Wednesday	Thursday	Friday	Saturday	Sunday
Mental Health	Hrs Activity	Hrs Activity	Hrs Activity	Hrs Activity	Hrs Activity	Hrs Activity	Hrs Activity
Relationships	Hrs Activity	Hrs Activity	Hrs Activity	Hrs Activity	Hrs Activity	Hrs Activity	Hrs Activity
Hobbies & Interests	Hrs Activity	Hrs Activity	Hrs Activity	Hrs Activity	Hrs Activity	Hrs Activity	Hrs Activity
Leisure and entertainment	Hrs Activity	Hrs Activity	Hrs Activity	Hrs Activity	Hrs Activity	Hrs Activity	Hrs Activity

Category	Monday	Tuesday	Wednesday	Thursday	Friday	Saturday	Sunday
Sleep	Hrs Activity	Hrs Activity	Hrs Activity	Hrs Activity	Hrs Activity	Hrs Activity	Hrs Activity
Household chores	Hrs Activity	Hrs Activity	Hrs Activity	Hrs Activity	Hrs Activity	Hrs Activity	Hrs Activity
Other	Hrs Activity	Hrs Activity	Hrs Activity	Hrs Activity	Hrs Activity	Hrs Activity	Hrs Activity

Step 2: Remove

Declutter and simplify, use the checklist below: Tick if Yes

1. **Have you decided when and how long?**
   Be clear on a specific time frame or duration for switching off from digital communication and physical clutter. This could be a few hours, a day, a weekend, or even a week. ☐

2. **Have you Informed others?**
   Let your friends, family, and colleagues know that you will be unavailable during this time. Set up an automated email response, update your social media status, or send out a message to inform people that you will not be responding to digital communication. ☐

3. **Have you set some boundaries?**
   Turn off notifications on your phone, tablet, and computer. Mute or put your devices on airplane mode to avoid distractions. Consider using a separate phone or device solely for emergencies, if necessary. ☐

4. **Have you cleared your physical space?**
   Declutter your immediate environment by organizing and tidying up. Put away items that are not needed or that contribute to visual clutter. Having a clean and organized space can help promote a sense of calm and focus. ☐

5. **Do you have a dedicated space to relax?**
   Designate a specific area in your home where you can relax and unwind. Make it comfortable and inviting by adding cushions, blankets, and soft lighting. This space can be used for reading, meditating, or simply enjoying some quiet time. ☐

Take time to reflect and recharge:

Use this time to reflect on your goals, values, and priorities. Journaling or practicing gratitude can help you gain clarity and perspective. Allow yourself to relax and recharge, both mentally and physically.

Step 3: Reset

Reflect on where you currently spend your time and what your current mindset is. Where would you like it to be? Use these questions as a prompt...

✓ **Am I constantly feeling overwhelmed and stressed by my workload?**

✓ **Do I frequently find myself unable to fully focus or be present due to the number of tasks I have?**

✓ **Is my busyness preventing me from engaging in activities or hobbies that bring me joy and fulfilment?**

✓ **How often do I prioritize self-care and relaxation amidst my busy schedule?**

✓ **Am I neglecting important relationships or failing to spend quality time (being present with them) with loved ones due to my busyness?**

✓ **Have I established clear goals and priorities to guide my actions or am I just constantly reacting to whatever comes my way?**

✓ **Are there areas of my life or work where I could delegate or ask for help to alleviate some of the busyness?**

✓ **Am I taking on tasks and responsibilities that align with my values and long-term goals or am I just saying yes to everything?**

✓ **How do I feel about the pace of my life and the level of busyness I am experiencing?**

✓ **What would I like to be different?**

✓ **What steps could I take to create more balance and reduce the busyness in my life?**

What are your reflections from the questions above?

____

____

____

____

____

____

Step 4: Resources

Support/accountability partner: Who can you call on to support you through this journey? Sharing where you are with someone means it is more likely that you will make the changes that are needed, and this, with a little consistency, is key when it comes to making positive changes. An accountability partner can help you stay consistent by reminding you of why you want to make changes, giving you feedback, and checking in on your progress regularly.

Meditation and mindfulness: Apps like Headspace and Calm offer guided meditation and mindfulness exercises that can help you take a break and find inner peace.

Nature: Spending time in nature can be incredibly rejuvenating. Take a walk in a park, go hiking, or simply sit outside and enjoy the fresh air and beauty of the natural world.

Books: Reading can be a great escape from a busy life. Choose a book that interests you and immerse yourself in its pages.

Yoga: Practicing yoga can help you relax, reduce stress, and find balance in your life. Many yoga studios offer classes for all levels, or you can find online tutorials and videos to practice at home.

Creative Outlets: Engaging in creative activities like painting, writing, or playing a musical instrument can provide a much-needed break and allow you to express yourself.

"I navigate the chaos like a boss,
turning mishaps into funny anecdotes.
I may not have a superpower,
but I wear a cape of laughter and
conquer each day with a smile"

— LISA POWNEY

3

Uncover

For as long as I can remember, until recent times, I have been "in search" of what I wanted in life: purpose, mission, wants, and desires included. Have you ever had that feeling of being in search of something but not really knowing what it is or what was driving you? I would keep myself constantly on the go, trying to prove myself but with no real clear direction, constantly drifting. A friend once said I was like flying on Concorde but with no destination. This was me for much of the time, but I also know that I have a secret superpower.

I'm married, and we have been together for 14 years now. We met when we were teenagers, 16 and 17 years old. At the time, I thought that I didn't really want children. I was frightened about being a good parent mostly, and I was ambitious. I had a husband who worked away all week, and I just couldn't see how I would fit it all in. Then, leading up to my 30th birthday, something hit me like a ton of bricks. I had this strong urge to have children. I guess some may call it the maternal instinct. My husband was very happy with the turnaround, and we started on our exciting journey to becoming parents.

A year in and nothing, and we started to worry. Worry turned into a reality... we found out we couldn't have children naturally. It hit us hard, and I don't know about you, but when I'm told that I can't have something, it becomes the thing I want more than anything!

It's results day. I haven't slept properly in days. I have been obsessed with looking into my pants for signs, and I'm exhausted. My husband is too. This IVF journey has been tough and taken its toll emotionally, more than anything I think I have experienced before. I woke up early, the darkness outside matching the heaviness in my heart. With trembling hands, I grabbed the pregnancy test that sat beside my bed. I made my way to the bathroom, and without uttering a word, my husband nodded in understanding.

It seems like forever for the test results to show, and in my heart, I know before I even look to see if there are two red lines the result. I pick it up, and silent tears flood down my face. All that hope, future dreams of being a family, dissolved by a wee on a stick. I open up the bathroom door, and he knows as soon as he looks at me. We stare at each other in silence for a while, not knowing what to say to each other. What do we do now? I crawl back into bed and hide my head under the duvet, hoping that sleep will take this pain away.

It never happened for us, and sadly, we ended up drifting apart and getting divorced.

So I'm single and thinking that maybe being a mum is not something that will happen to me. For a while, I was okay with that, and then I went on a retreat with a great friend of mine at the time. It was an amazing week of juicing, meditation, yoga, exercise, and being with wonderful people. Throughout the week, people started to have their own meltdowns and end up in tears, often because they had landed on their own epiphany. I, however, felt that I was resistant to this. Life was pretty good, and I was having a lovely time, learning lots from all of it. So I remember thinking, "Well, that's not going to happen to me." So on the evening of the final day, I'm shocked to find myself in floods of tears, jumping on a trampoline overlooking the edge of a beautiful mountain.

At the end of the trampette session, my lovely friend notices my tears and takes me to sit at the edge. She kindly asks me what's going on, and without thinking, I blurt out, "I really want to be a mum." The desire and knowing were beyond anything I have ever felt before and probably since. From that day, I got into action. I had such clarity about my next steps, and I could visualize and feel every day what being a mum would look, feel, and sound like.

I went on a very interesting journey to become a mum, and I think there is a book on this itself. However, I finally settled on the fact that I would try IVF again but this time as a single mum. This felt liberating and purposeful, and I started nesting before it even was a possibility. I turned down a promotion. I remember my boss saying, "Ok, great you want a baby. Are you with anyone, Lis?" At the time, I wasn't, but that didn't phase me. I sold my smaller house and bought a bigger one. I swapped my car and booked my flight to Barcelona to get the process started.

It's nearing the end of the year, and I'm all set up and ready to go full throttle in the New Year. I'm living with my mum while I wait for the new house to be built. It's between Christmas and New Year, and I'm sitting on the sofa after having an emotional breakdown with mum, worrying that this plan might not work (still can kick in even if you know that's what you desperately want, by the way!) when I get a text out of the blue from the first person I ever dated. He was older than me, and my mum didn't like it, so she made it come to an end. We ended up meeting, and although I didn't immediately connect back with him, we did over a few weeks and eventually became a couple. He had never had children due to unforeseen circumstances in his life, and of course, I hadn't either. But with only a few months together, we found ourselves pregnant with our wonderful miracle boy, Freddie. No IVF needed; it happened as I knew in my heart and my head it would.

When I truly find something I desire and can align my feelings, thoughts, and experiences to, it happens! Something innate in me provides hyperfocus and clarity, where I am able to visualise and articulate what I want with precision, and then I'm on it. So, I know I have this superpower, so why don't I use it all the time? Well, for me, and maybe for you, the hard part is defining that desire and getting clarity on where you are now, so you know which direction to take. That's where the second step – **uncover** – comes in.

So what do I mean by **Uncover**? At the time of writing this book, I'm a very proud single older mum of a beautiful boy, with the energy of a Duracell bunny whose batteries NEVER run out. He's constantly on the go, constantly asking questions, constantly wanting to do the next thing, and I wouldn't change a thing! I have a full-time career leading a Learning consultancy team as well as being a life coach and breathwork teacher outside of this. I am also managing a household in this tough financial climate, exercising, losing weight, and learning to be a better speaker. So, you might have guessed, like my son, I'm the type of person that is always on the move, rushing from one task to another, and feeling overwhelmed by the never-ending to-do lists that seem to control my life. My friends and work colleagues often challenge me to slow down, to stop proving myself as some kind of 'superwoman'.

This isn't new; it's something I have done for years. On previous occasions, as a result of my constant hustle and inability to slow down, my body would finally give in and force me to confront my own limitations. Burnout would hit me like a ton of bricks, leaving me physically and mentally exhausted. The last time this happened, it was more serious than ever before, and I realised it was a wake-up call that I couldn't ignore.

For the first time in a long time, I had no choice but to pause and reassess my priorities. I realized that constantly pushing myself to the limit was not sustainable, and it was taking a toll on my well-being. I had neglected self-care and failed to listen to the signals my body was sending me. During my recovery, I had a lot of time to reflect on my life and the choices I had made. I began to question whether being constantly busy and achieving more and more was truly fulfilling. I started to understand that true success and happiness were not solely defined by what I could accomplish in a day.

I had become so consumed by busyness, and I needed to understand what was driving this so that I could address it and move forward. It was clear that I was spreading myself too thin and it was causing me to lose control of my time. I started by reassessing my priorities and identifying the activities that truly brought joy and fulfilment to me. It wasn't easy breaking old habits and letting go of the need to constantly prove myself. But with each small step I took towards a more balanced and fulfilling life, I felt a sense of liberation and peace.

So today, although I have all that going on, I have learned to embrace the moments of stillness and prioritise self-care. I have come to understand that taking care of myself is not selfish but necessary in order to be the best version of myself for my son and for others. I have also shifted my perspective on success. It is no longer about achieving more and more, but about finding joy and fulfilment in the present moment. I have discovered the power of slowing down and savouring the simple pleasures in life. I am grateful for the lesson's burnout taught me. It was a harsh wake-up call that forced me to re-evaluate my priorities and make positive changes. Today, I am more resilient, grounded, and focused on living a life that is balanced and aligned with my values.

So, to all those who challenge me to slow down and stop trying to be a "superwoman," I now respond with a smile and a grateful heart. I have learned that being kind to myself and taking time to focus on the root cause of my busyness is essential because once you have this, you can start to address these underlying causes, regain control of your time, and move forward on your journey to a more balanced life.

There are a number of ways you can do this. I like to use my **Personal Assessment Principles** to help get to the root cause of both what's causing your busyness and what you desire.

The first task I would recommend as a prep for this step would be to identify your values and priorities: Reflect on what truly matters to you in life.

One of my favourite films that I like to watch with my son, Freddie, is "Inside Out" (2015). I don't know if you have seen it, but it's a great watch for kids and adults alike. This film focuses on the inner emotions of a young girl named Riley. Joy, Sadness, Fear, Anger, and Disgust live inside her mind at the Headquarters of her emotions. The emotions control Riley's actions and memories, and they work together to guide her through life. You see Riley move to a new city with her family and struggle with her emotions. There are lots of lessons you can learn from this, and for me in particular, there is one scene where "Joy," who wants Riley to always be happy, explains the importance of core memories. These memories come from a super important time in Riley's life. She tells us how each core memory powers a different aspect of Riley's personality and describes each of them as an island. There's 'Hockey Island,' 'Goofball island,' 'friendship island,' 'love honesty island' (not the TV reality version!), and 'family island.' She explains that the point is the islands of personality are what make Riley, Riley! There's a lovely portrayal of these core memories being sent to long-term memory for her to access whenever she needs to know what is important to her and what makes her happy. It brings to life for me the significance of reflecting on joyful memories and the impact they have on shaping one's emotions and overall well-being. At the time of writing this, the sequel will be out shortly, and I can't wait to watch it!

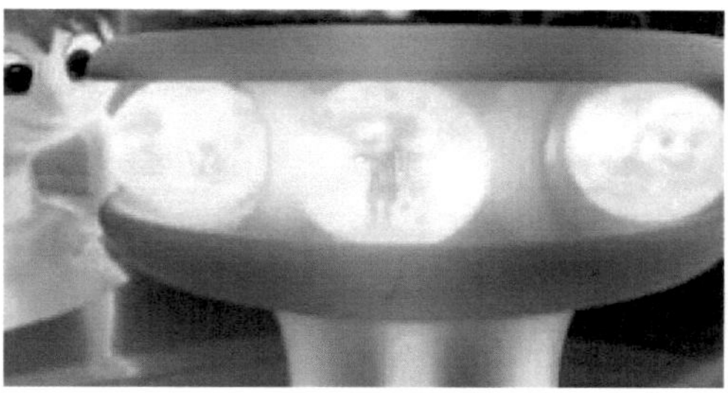

So, with this film in mind, it's important as a preparation step to take some time to think about your life and experiences. Reflect on the moments that have brought you the most joy, fulfilment, and satisfaction.

Consider the activities, relationships, and accomplishments that have felt meaningful and aligned with who you are. Use this to identify your core beliefs. What themes can you take from this thinking? What guiding principles resonate with you?

The P.E.R.S.O.N.A.L Assessment Principles

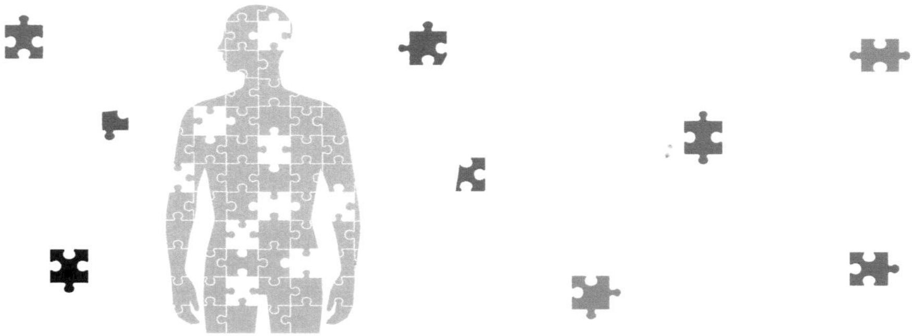

P.E.R.S.O.N.A.L Assessment principles **Give yourself a score 1-10 for each of these in the puzzle and write why**
Physical - This section focuses on your physical health. Are you taking care of your body? What is the overall state of your physical well-being, including fitness, nutrition, sleep, and general health? Consider factors such as your exercise routine, diet, and any existing health issues.
Emotional - This section addresses your emotional health. How are you taking care of your emotional well-being, including self-awareness, emotional intelligence, stress management, and resilience? Reflect on your ability to handle and express emotions effectively.

Relationships - When was the last time you assessed the quality of your relationships with family, friends, colleagues, and significant others? Consider factors such as communication, trust, support, and the overall health of your connections.

Self-Esteem - This refers to the overall opinion and evaluation that an individual has about themselves. Having healthy self-esteem is crucial for personal growth, happiness, and success in various aspects of life. How positive do you feel about your self-image and self-worth?

Origin - This provides insight into a person's background, upbringing, and past experiences, which can greatly influence their current beliefs, behaviours, and thinking patterns. How has your family background influenced your beliefs and behaviours? Are there any beliefs or patterns that you would like to change or redefine? Are there any past traumas or unresolved issues that are still impacting your present life? How can you heal and move forward? Are there any self-limiting beliefs or negative patterns that need to be challenged and reframed? This self-awareness can pave the way for personal growth, healing, and the creation of a more fulfilling and purposeful life.

Northstar - This section focuses on your life vision and purpose. Do you have clarity and alignment with your life vision and purpose? Consider your goals, dreams, values, and the overall direction of your life.

Abundance - Abundance is an important topic within the coaching realm of life. It refers to the concept of having an abundance mindset, which is the belief that there is more than enough of everything in the world for everyone to thrive and succeed. This includes financial abundance but is much broader than that. Do you have an abundance mindset?

Life - This section is about having a fulfilling life. As an individual, do you prioritize your enjoyment, pursue your passions, and focus on creating a more fulfilling life? Are you clear on what truly brings you joy? Do you set aside time for those things that make you happy? Do you have a good work-life balance?

Now you have scored this:

✓ **Which of these areas are the most important for you?**

✓ **Where does there feel like there is a sense of urgency?**

✓ **How do the scores compare to the amount of time you dedicate to them?**

Now you have answered these what do you feel are your priorities that need to change to give you a more balanced life?

"The Art of Selflessness: get wet in the rain to keep others dry"

— LISA POWNEY

4

Manifest

Do as I say, not as I do…

As alluded to in the previous chapter, I have always been the type of person who says "Yes" to opportunities, experiences, or the needs of others. I'm the ultimate "faddy." I remember coming home from a brilliant trip to China with my case loaded with new things to fit into my already very busy schedule for that year. In the next few months, I was getting married, moving home, and settling into a new job…not busy enough! As I unpacked my suitcase filled with treasures from China, I couldn't help but feel a mix of excitement. Each item, as it always does to me, represented a new opportunity, a new experience, and I often think to myself, "This could be it, I have finally found 'The Thing!'" But deep down, I knew that my already busy schedule had no gaps in it for fitting in this as well. In the first days, the enthusiasm got me to make some time "in between" meetings, household chores, and visiting family to have a go at this newfound wisdom I had. The bat and ball went first; I discovered that I had no technique, and the ball often landed on my head, so that got put down. The calligraphy was next; I remember writing my sister a card with some random Chinese letters and told her it was "Good luck" in Chinese. I had no clue. Finally, I reviewed the cards for a few days, but they too were laid down. The items laid down on the kitchen table for a good few weeks before being moved to the garage and not seen again until I moved. Brilliant!

In addition to being "faddy," I had always prided myself on being the ultimate people pleaser too. Saying yes to every opportunity that came my way had become second nature to me. Whether it was taking on extra projects at work, volunteering for various organisations, or simply being there for friends and family, I never hesitated to show up. But having struggled through another week, I reflected on finding myself stretched thin, constantly overcommitted, and exhausted. I was resentful and began to question if my eagerness to please others was actually serving me.

I'm a facilitator and deliver lots of different content for our clients. One of my favourite modules is resilience, and as I usually do, I talked about our "stress cup." Just like a cup can only hold a certain amount of liquid, a person's stress cup represents their ability to manage stressors in their life. This simple reminder, although I had spoken about it many times before, prompted the thought that I needed to prioritise my own well-being and happiness before constantly trying to please others.

So, what is driving this ineffective way of thinking and being? Amongst other things, I now know that my desire to please people stems from having it as a survival mechanism during childhood, constantly on high alert, trying to second-guess what I needed to do in order to please my father. Through therapy conversations, I have come to realise that my younger self, Lisa, would finish every day thinking about what she could do differently the next day to please her father and make the situation right, hoping that he would be happy and not hurt us anymore. This created a thought pattern from an early age that my attempts to please could somehow change how someone else behaves towards me. Talking it through, I now realize that this need to please was just a way for me to reduce the risk of rejection and all the feelings of low self-worth, shame, and insecurity that it always brings. Additionally, this thought pattern has also made it difficult for me in the past to set limits, say "no," or assert my own needs; I have learned to prioritise others' desires and emotions.

Sorry, I can't come to your rescue; I'm busy saving myself.

It was time for a change. I decided to embark on a journey of self-discovery and self-care. I started by setting boundaries and learning to say **NO** when necessary. I realised that by saying "yes" to everything, I was spreading myself too thin and sacrificing my own happiness. I needed to prioritise my time and energy for the things that truly mattered to me. As I became more attuned to my own needs, I discovered that being a people pleaser didn't define me. I learned that it was okay to disappoint others occasionally, as long as I was true to myself and prioritised my own well-being.

To really make this count, I had to make a conscious decision to evaluate my priorities and set some boundaries. It was clear that my desire to say "yes" to everything was taking a toll on my well-being. I needed to find a balance that allowed me to continue pursuing opportunities and meeting the needs of others while also taking care of myself.

Reflecting on my values and what truly mattered to me now in **UNCOVER**. I realised that my own personal growth, health, and happiness were just as important as meeting the needs of others. With this newfound clarity, I started to prioritise my own well-being and set limits on the commitments I would take on. At the time, I had a young son and a busy job with lots of potential for career growth. However, I knew I had to make a decision that allowed me to be a mum and put that first for a while. I talked to my work and explained my need to scale back. It wasn't an easy conversation, as I didn't want to let them down, but I knew it was necessary for my own sanity. They were understanding and supportive, recognising that I needed to take care of myself first. I began to declutter my schedule and started planning scheduled time for activities for myself first. By doing this, I learned to say no when I felt overwhelmed. I knew that by doing so, I was actually taking better care of myself and preserving my energy for the things that truly mattered to me. Over time, I have found that by setting boundaries and making self-care a priority, I am able to be more present and engaged in the opportunities and experiences I choose to pursue. I no longer feel the constant pressure to say yes to everything. Instead, I aim to focus on the ones that align with my values and bring me genuine fulfilment. I don't always get it right. It is a continuous process of self-discovery and learning. But I recognise the early signs and go back to my framework to get it right.

So now, when I think about the case filled with treasures from China, I smile. Each item represents a lesson learned, a reminder of the importance of finding balance and saying yes to myself as much as I say yes to others. And as I move forward, I know that my journey will continue to evolve, guided by the wisdom gained from embracing both opportunities and self-care.

So what do I mean by Manifest?

I first crossed paths with Emma during my third round job interview, a decade ago. From the moment we met, there was an undeniable connection. We bonded over our recent escapades in Ibiza and our independent lives as single professionals. Since then, we have become the best of friends, embarking on countless adventures and accumulating stories that could fill a book. Emma is an extraordinary individual – kind, caring, beautiful, and incredibly intelligent. Although we match on these traits ha ha, in many ways, we are complete opposites. But that's what makes our friendship so special. We often laugh about our differences. I remember as my line manager, during a 1:1 meeting, she asked me if I had done an activity, and I replied, "I'm not there yet, but for me, it's all about the journey." She quickly replied, "F**k the journey, it's **All** about the destination. Get it done!" Ha ha ha ...

Now, let me tell you why Emma is such an exceptional person. She possesses an unparalleled talent for organisation, setting boundaries, and prioritising her time. People find comfort in her ability to say "no" to non-essential tasks and commitments. If you ever have the chance to ask Emma to demonstrate her system of managing time, you'll be blown away by its brilliance. I keep urging her to write a book about it! Emma understands the value of time unlike anyone else. She recognises that it is a finite resource that cannot be replenished and, therefore, must be used wisely. Her philosophy revolves around making intentional choices, prioritising what truly matters, and maximising the value of the time we have. Emma plans meticulously, crafting an annual schedule, detailed weekly schedules, and daily reviews. What sets her apart is that she prioritises self-care and relationships above all else. Once she commits to something, she follows through with unwavering dedication. This mindset and practical application have greatly contributed to her success.

Fairness is Emma's guiding principle, rooted in her strong core values. She constantly sets limits on her availability and the time she invests in various activities and relationships. With a high level of self-awareness, she effortlessly creates boundaries in her work, personal time, and social commitments. Emma's calendar is her bible – not only does she plan meticulously, but she also remains disciplined and consistent. She holds herself accountable for her actions. It's no wonder she is the most productive person I've ever encountered – and I absolutely adore it!

Despite her incredible achievements, Emma can be really hard on herself if she falls short of her commitments, whether to herself or others. We often discuss the importance of embracing our humanity and giving ourselves a break. She truly is awesome.

You too can take steps towards Emma through Manifest.

Manifest is all about setting your new boundaries, going after what you want and brings you joy, and just as importantly, turning down and saying 'No' to the things that you don't want.

Manifest

Calm Cadence Creator
Concentrate – Your overall strategy at this stage is to **concentrate on your priorities** identified in the previous step. The key to maintaining focus and dedicating your time and energy to what truly matters is to articulate your priorities in a way that allows you to assess progress and make adjustments as needed.
Core - While your priorities determine **what** you want to achieve, your core values guide **how** you approach them. Your core values serve as a compass, influencing your actions and decisions in pursuing your priorities. Aligning boundaries in the next step with your values can help you determine how to allocate your time and energy.

Create – This stage is about creating new boundaries around your priorities. Take the time to identify your personal, emotional, and physical boundaries in relation to your priorities. Understand what you are willing and unwilling to accept or do in certain situations. It's crucial to have a strategy for dealing with boundary crossings and to consider the consequences of others' actions.
Concede– Achieving a better work-life balance may require sacrificing some activities and lower priorities. Clearly understanding what you are willing to give up can lead to increased satisfaction and fulfilment. It allows you to allocate time and energy to activities and relationships that are important to you.
Calendar - Your calendar becomes your new best friend in this process. Use it effectively by regularly planning, following through with discipline, creating routines through consistency, and holding yourself accountable to your commitments and responsibilities. With proper planning, discipline, consistency, and accountability, your calendar can truly support you in achieving your goals and maintaining a balanced and productive life.
Compassion – Setting boundaries can be challenging, especially if it's not something you're used to. Be patient with yourself and practice self-compassion. It's okay to make adjustments along the way and learn from any experiences that arise.

So let me tell you about my oh-so-exciting love life. Or should I say, lack thereof? Yeah, you heard me right. I've been flying solo for a solid 5 YEARS! But hey, who's counting, right? Now, let me share with you the one positive thing about my singledom – I don't have to worry about trimming my lady garden on a regular basis. Well, except for that one time when I had a hospital appointment. I knew they were going to stick a massive cucumber-sized rod up there, so I figured I'd make it presentable.

Back in the day, when I was still on the market, I made a wise investment in laser hair removal. I endured endless hours of pain to make sure my legs and armpits were as smooth as a baby's bottom. And boy, did it pay off! I may not have gone swimming except on holidays, but the freedom of not having to shave my legs every time I wanted to take a dip was a real delight.

Now, as for getting my nether regions "lasered," let's just say I only braved that torture a couple of times. It hurt like hell, and that was the end of that crazy idea. But here's the thing. One day, I went to my laser session, thinking it would be a routine affair. Little did I know what awaited me. I walked into the room, and there she was – the beautician. Picture-perfect, with her perfectly coiffed hair, long lashes, and flawless makeup. And she casually drops the bombshell, "Hey, want me to take care of the hair around your bottom too? It's become quite popular, you know."

I was dumbfounded. Hair around my bottom? Are you kidding me? I've been dating for years and never knew I had this problem! So, in a state of shock, I blurted out, "Uh, sure, why not?" Next thing I know, I'm pants-less, on all fours on a salon bed, while the beautician trims my bum hair with a comb and scissors. Let me tell you, I've never been more embarrassed in my life. And to top it all off, she proceeds to unleash the most excruciating laser treatment I've ever experienced. I'm in pain, mortified, and practically butt-naked with a stranger working on my rear end. And all the while, she's trying to make small talk about parking problems in the town. That was it for me. No more bikini or bum work, thank you very much. Why can't I learn to say NO!

Once you have taken the steps in **Manifest**, it automatically becomes much easier to say **No** to the things that no longer serve you or bring you joy. I found it really helpful to take on board that saying no didn't make me a bad person or mean that I was neglecting others. In fact, it allowed me to show up more fully and authentically when I did say yes. By setting boundaries and being selective about the commitments

I took on, I was able to give my best self to each opportunity. This not only benefits me but also the people and causes I choose to support. We will talk more about communicating your boundaries and saying No in the right way in the next step.

Progressing on all of these steps collectively requires a holistic approach to personal growth and self-management. Here are some ways to make progress on each step:

1. Concentrate:

✓ **From the previous steps take your top priority and note down all the tasks that need to be done to achieve this priority. Write down every task that comes to mind, without worrying about the order or organization at this stage.**

✓ **Now try to group them. Are there any obvious categories?**

✓ **Prioritise each task in this Impact - Effort matrix (Eisenhower matrix)**

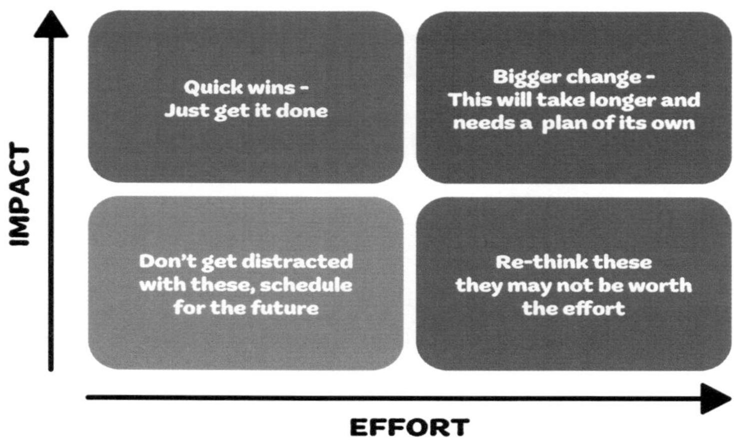

✓ **Identify the one task you are going to work on first.**

✓ **What are your first 3 steps you can do towards achieving this task?**

Set a specific time to do these and measurable milestones to track your progress.

2. Care:

✓ **What self-care activities can you incorporate into your daily routine, such as exercise, meditation, or hobbies?**

✓ **What would doing these do for you?**

3. Core:

✓ **Think about a moment in your work life when you felt most fulfilled, satisfied, and alive. Write it out without thinking about it too much.**

✓ **Now reflect on your writing, are there any words or themes that jump out at you?**

- ✓ **Think about a moment in your personal life when you felt most fulfilled, satisfied, and alive. Write it out without thinking about it too much.**

- ✓ **Now reflect on your writing, are there any words or themes that jump out at you?**

✓ **Think about a childhood moment when you felt at your happiest. Write it out without thinking about it too much.**

✓ **Now reflect on your writing, are there any words or themes that jump out at you?**

✓ **Consider your natural talents, skills, and strengths. What activities or areas of life allow you to fully utilize these strengths?**

✓ **Ask trusted friends, family members, or mentors what they believe your core values are based on their observations of your behaviour and choices.**

✓ **Now having done that, what is this telling you about your values?**

4. Boundaries:

✓ **Look back to when you began this journey. What were the reasons that brought you here? What made you start? What were you doing that made you feel unhappy? What does this teach you about the limits you need to set for yourself?**

✓ **What changes do you need to make to your schedule to keep to your boundaries?**

✓ **Who will you need to communicate these boundaries to?**

5. Concede:

✓ **Evaluate your commitments and activities that you recorded in the Halt step. Are there any here that are not aligned with your priorities right now?**

✓ **How willing are you to let go of these to create space for what truly matters? What, if anything, is stopping you?**

✓ **What are you willing to let go of right now?**

6. Calendar:

✓ **Open your calendar or planner to schedule and organise your tasks and activities. Based on the above, prioritise your time and allocate it according to your priorities first.**

✓ **Review this now, what are your feelings about it? Does it feel realistic? Does it bring any sense of relief? Make any adjustments.**

✓ **Develop a habit of adhering to your calendar and holding yourself accountable to your scheduled tasks.**

7. Compassion:

✓ **Set a weekly evaluation point and check-in, and ask yourself, how does it feel?**

✓ **Be patient with yourself as you navigate through the process of setting and enforcing boundaries.**

✓ **Learn from your experiences and use them as opportunities for growth and improvement.**

✓ **Seek support and guidance from others who can offer compassion and understanding.**

✓ **By integrating these strategies and consistently working on each step, you can make progress collectively and create a more balanced and fulfilling life. Remember, personal growth is a journey, so be patient and celebrate each step forward.**

"I might look like I'm not taking action but in my head I'm really busy"

— LISA POWNEY

5

Activate

From a young age, you would often find me lost in my own world of daydreams, seeking solace and imagining a better life at home. In my mind, I painted vivid pictures of my parents finding happiness and my father transforming into a kind and loving person, realising the errors of his ways. These dreams portrayed a "normal" family, filled with safety, happiness, and security—a stark departure from the reality we lived in. Occasionally, I would share these dreams with my sisters, and it became our secret superpower, helping us cope with the harshness of our circumstances.

As time went on, I discovered that all three of us had developed our own unique superpowers to navigate the challenges we faced. While I have always cherished the bond we share as sisters, I now realise just how extraordinary they truly are. This superpower of mine has accompanied me throughout my life, providing solace and aiding me in coping with various situations. However, I have also come to understand that it has held me back, preventing me from taking action to change my circumstances.

Instead of confronting the harsh realities, I would often bury my head under the covers, seeking refuge in my dreams, convinced that one day, everything would effortlessly fall into place. As I grew older, my dreams became more elaborate, envisioning a life where I started my own business, embarked on exciting travels, and found the love of my life. These fantasies brought me a fleeting sense of fulfilment and happiness. I would even go as far as planning the necessary steps to make these dreams a reality. Yet, when it came down to taking action and facing the uncertainties and challenges that lie ahead, I would retreat into my dreams once again, using them as a shield to avoid moving forward.

Now, I recognise that my reliance on these dreams has kept me stagnant for far too long. It is time for me to break free from their allure and confront the world head-on. While my dreams have provided temporary comfort, they have also hindered my growth and prevented me from embracing the unknown. I finally realised with the help of two amazing women who go by the names of Cheryl Chapman and Jane Leonard @Confidently come speaking that it was time to step out from under the duvet, face reality, and take the necessary steps to create the life I desire. Only then can I truly experience the excitement, safety, and fulfilment I have always yearned for.

Do you feel a strong connection with any of these words? Are you ready to break free from mere dreams and wishes and dive headfirst into action? If you've made it this far, you're already 60% closer to your goal. Push through this barrier, because it's at this point that winners are truly born. For me, Activate is more than just action because it encompasses a deeper level of engagement and commitment. When we activate ourselves, we not only take physical action, but we also tap into our inner motivation and harness our full potential. Activation involves aligning our thoughts, emotions, and actions towards a specific goal or purpose. It requires us to push through obstacles, overcome doubts and fears, and stay persistent in the face of challenges. By activating ourselves, we bring a higher level of intention and energy to our actions, making them more meaningful and impactful. So, activation goes beyond mere action by infusing it with passion, purpose, and resilience.

What do I mean by Activate?

If I had to think of someone who embodies activation, it would undoubtedly be Jane Leonard, an extraordinary woman I've had the pleasure of working with when I joined the brilliant Confidently Come Speaking community. Jane is a force of nature like no other. She served in the military, represented England in rugby, and even holds a world record. But what sets her apart is her unwavering commitment to taking action, no matter what. Jane has been a profound and positive influence in my recent life, pushing me to believe in myself and inspiring me to write this book. I am immensely grateful for her presence.

One of Jane's favourite sayings is "Plan the Dive, Dive the Plan." Initially, this concept felt foreign to me, as I have always had a penchant for procrastination. If procrastination were a skill, I would be a master. However, when I truly embraced this ethos, I discovered that it was liberating rather than restrictive. It eliminated the room for indecisiveness because when we give ourselves choices, we also give ourselves the option to let ourselves off or make the wrong ones. By meticulously planning and wholeheartedly following through, we can truly make a difference.

Thanks to this newfound mindset, I have achieved remarkable personal milestones. I have shed 3 stone in weight, lost significant inches, developed a love for exercise, and embarked on the journey of writing this book. Additionally, I have had the privilege of learning from the incredible Cheryl Chapman and honing my skills as a speaker. Activation has transformed my life in ways I never thought possible, and I owe much of it to Jane and her unwavering belief in taking decisive action.

Under Activate, I use my four steps Positive Performance P.L.A.N.

Keep your beliefs limiting - who's got time, really, for taking risks or jumping on opportunities?

During a phase of being unattached, I didn't have to worry about snoring or wearing mismatched pyjamas to bed. And let me tell you, my favourite underwear mysteriously transformed into these so-called "Shorts" from M&S. They're basically oversized pants pretending to be shorts. Do you know what I mean? My mum predicted this would happen – I have officially surrendered to the comfort of elasticated trousers and the charm of M&S fashion. Who would've guessed?

Amidst this period of apathy and fear of being single forever, the thought of diving back into the dating scene is absolutely terrifying. But then, on one seemingly insignificant day, while satisfying my caffeine cravings at the Starbucks drive-thru, something extraordinary unfolded. Opting for a cappuccino, the "healthier" choice, I pulled up to the window and caught sight of a mesmerizing individual standing there.

They possessed undeniable attractiveness, exuded strength, and had dark hair, olive skin, and a smile that could melt hearts. I couldn't help but be captivated. And to my astonishment, they caught me staring and responded with the most enchanting smile. I quickly averted my gaze, but then I remembered the golden rule of flirting – maintain eye contact. So, I summoned the courage to look back, and they mouthed the words, "Hello, how are you?"

I pointed to myself, utterly dumbfounded, and mouthed, "Me?" Can you believe it? This stunning person actually wanted to engage in conversation with me! They nodded and confirmed, "Yes, you. How are you?" I managed to stammer out a response, and all of this unfolded in what felt like an eternity, but in reality, it was mere minutes as the barista prepared their croissant and my coffee. With one final smile, they grabbed their croissant and gracefully made their way to a table.

As I waited for my coffee, a feeling of pure elation washed over me, as if I was floating on cloud nine. As I drove away, passing by the window, they smiled and waved. Naturally, I eagerly reciprocated with a smile and wave of my own, but in my excitement, I accidentally veered onto the pavement, narrowly avoiding a collision with a post… How typical! How utterly brilliant! Mortified, I continued driving, yet a smile crept upon my face. Wait, could it be? I think I just felt a glimmer of belief! For the next 6 months you would find me working at said 'Starbucks' just in case and those M & S pants have gone out of the window.

Sometimes, all it takes is a mere glimmer… Just a tiny spark of belief can be like sprinkling magical dust on your dreams… and that's when things get interesting. Because those seemingly insignificant sparks have the power to ignite unwavering self-confidence and guide us towards achieving our deepest desires and ultimate success! Isn't it exhilaratingly scary?

So before we enter the next step let's get our head in the right space and explore if you have had any recent glimmers of belief?

Note down when recently did you experience any of the following symptoms?

✓ **Positive Expectations** - A time when you have found yourself expecting a bit of a positive outcome or envisioning the possibility of success

✓ **Increased confidence** – A time when you have experienced even a small boost in self – confidence.

✓ **Some motivation** - A time when you have felt a moment of inspiration or motivation to take action

✓ **Decrease in self-doubt** - A time when you have noticed a little less self-doubt about something in your life.

✓ **Optimism** - A time when you felt the initial shoots of optimism about overcoming a challenge or obstacle

✓ **Feeling in the flow** - A time when you have felt some kind of emotional connection and a sense of ease with something

If you have found evidence for any of the above, now is time to celebrate the small wins. Give yourself a Whoop Whoop! And for those of you where it's too much, give yourself a well done...

Let's build on this and see if this Positive Performance Plan can ignite more than just a glimmer in you....

Activate

Positive Performance P.L.A.N
Priorities - Unlocking your potential to conquer your **priorities** hinges on cultivating a mindset that propels you to deliver. To embark on this transformative journey, it is vital to grasp the "Why" - the purpose that fuels your actions. By envisioning what success truly entails and embracing the profound changes it brings, you can navigate the path towards a purposeful existence. Here, you are looking to ignite the fire within to conquer your priorities.
Limits - Are there any limiting beliefs that could hold you back and stop you from delivering on your priorities? What can you do to minimize, question, and challenge these beliefs to determine if they truly serve you? Replace them with empowering beliefs that support your alignment with your priorities and propel you forward. As you continue to take action, pay attention to your thoughts, emotions, and actions throughout the day.
Actions - Take intentional action to break down your priorities into the smallest, most actionable steps and consistently take those steps. Align your daily actions with your priorities to ensure you are making progress towards what matters most to you. It's important to focus on one action at a time and move on to the next one. Regularly review your progress and make adjustments as needed.
Nail it - Taking intentional action requires discipline and focus to succeed. This is about staying committed to your actions and reminding yourself of the benefits of aligning your actions with what truly matters to you. In this stage, it's vital to celebrate small wins along the way to stay motivated and maintain momentum.

Positive Performance P.L.A.N

Priorities

✓ **The reason I am wanting to make this change is...?**

✓ **I will know I will be successful when...?**

✓ **When this change happens, my life will be different in the following ways...**

Limits

✓ **Take a few moments to think about your priorities, are there any limiting beliefs that could hold you back and stop you delivering on your priorities? Note them down here...**

✓ **Now go back and next to them replace them with empowering beliefs that support your alignment with your priorities and propel you forward.**

Actions

Identify the 3 smallest actions you are going to take to move you closer to your priorities

Action 1	Action 2	Action 3

Nail it

✓ **What small wins can you celebrate on this journey so far?**

"I have mastered the Art of Falling Off the Wagon and blaming it on my 'Other' Me"

— LISA POWNEY

6

Nurture

I mentioned being on a retreat in Uncover. This happened a number of years ago when I was assigned to a new client. I entered the office and immediately came across someone I had met before in my previous organization. Lisa smiled and continued with her work. However, over the next couple of days, we would laugh and chat, and by the end of the week, we had agreed to go on a well-being retreat in Turkey together! It formed a great friendship, and we had so many fun times together. We discovered spirituality and leaned on each other for support. So, we embarked on our new adventure to this juice retreat, and I remember asking Lisa at the airport, "So, what do you think we should expect? No food, only juice, lots of exercise, and yoga... What? No food!!!!!!! What had I booked?"

We arrived, and it was a magical place high up on a mountain in Turkey. The air was filled with the refreshing scent of freshly squeezed juices, and the serene landscape seemed to radiate positive energy. We were both really giddy about the experience.

During our stay, we immersed ourselves in the various activities and practices offered at the mountain. We embraced the power of juicing, practiced yoga, and meditated to find inner peace. The supportive community inspired us, and we had long conversations with each other and others committed to making positive changes in our lives. We absolutely loved the feeling of being in control of our health and well-being, and although challenged by the lack of food, we definitely

Me making the most of the airport before no food and drink for a week!!!!

felt more energised and alive than ever before. I felt that my mindset had definitely shifted—boom!

When we returned from the mountain, both being faddy, we bought every bit of equipment that juicing could ever require, along with yoga mats and even a trampette!!! And for the first week or so, we kept most of it up. The reality was, though, we had to deal with our everyday life. The demands of work, family, and social obligations began to take a toll on us. Temptation lurked around every corner, and slowly but surely, we found ourselves succumbing to old habits, making every excuse under the sun!

I jumped off the wagon and indulged in unhealthy food choices and neglected much of my well-being. I remember feeling disappointed in myself for losing the momentum I had gained at the mountain. I tried to get back on track a number of times, but my efforts felt futile, and I struggled to regain my motivation. It got worse...

My disappointment grew, and I started doubting my ability to make lasting changes. I felt discouraged and became overwhelmed by the challenges I faced. The allure of my old lifestyle seemed irresistible, and I began to question if my time at the mountain had been a waste of time in a well-being sense.

Why choose this particular story? It serves as a powerful lesson in diligently following the right path, experiencing a transformative shift in perspective, but ultimately faltering before you have the chance to fully cultivate it into a lasting habit. However, it's not only that which will knock you off your pedestal....In the recent times, I embarked on an incredible 3-month journey of self-discovery, wellness, and personal growth. It all began when I joined a captivating mindset, health, and fitness program led by Jane, whom I mentioned earlier. The programme aimed to ignite the fire within each participant, guiding us towards our aspirations throughout the festive season and into the promising embrace of the new year. As the first month unfolded, I felt an unwavering determination coursing through my veins. Eagerly, I immersed myself in every session, embracing the challenges and triumphing over the daily goals. A sense of fulfilment and joy washed over me, like a warm, comforting embrace.

However, halfway through this transformative month, I found myself in a bit of a funk. It was one of those Friday mornings when a 6 am call awaited me. I woke up with the dawn, but a wave of resistance washed over me. I whispered to myself, "I'm just not feeling it today." Excuses began to dance in my mind, tempting me to bail on the meeting, with the promise of watching the recording later. Yet, deep down, I knew that I would regret such a decision. So, despite my initial hesitation, I made a conscious choice to not join this time.

The programme operated on a points system. Attending sessions live rewarded us with two points, while watching the replays earned us one point. I mustered the courage to face my disappointment when I received only a single point for that missed session. Nevertheless, I made a resolute decision to show up for every other opportunity that came my way. And show up I did, with unwavering dedication and unwavering commitment. As the month ended, the moment arrived to announce the victor. Alas, fate did not choose me as the champion. Fair enough, the lady who emerged victorious undoubtedly deserved the recognition. Yet, it stung to realise that I had missed out on the grand prize by a mere one point! Just one point stood between me and a much needed £250, an amount that could have alleviated the post-Christmas financial strain. The disappointment lingered, leaving a bittersweet taste in my mouth.

So, what lesson can we glean from this experience? It is a simple yet profound truth: Show up! Even when your heart resists, even when the path seems arduous, even when you don't feel like it. For in those moments of doubt and reluctance, lies the potential for tremendous growth and unforeseen impact. It is in showing up, against all odds, that we truly discover the depths of our resilience and the heights of our potential.

So what can we do to avoid these pitfalls I have very much fallen in? The final step to my bounce back recovery program is **Nurture**.

What do I mean by Nurture?

Back in the day, I was a branch manager at a building society. I started off as a financial advisor, and that's when I crossed paths with my crazy and beautiful friend, Laura. Let me tell you, everyone adores Laura. She's funny, flirty, smart, and kind. She's hands down one of the best people I've ever worked with, and trust me, I've had the pleasure of working with some really special people.

According to Laura, every Friday at the branch was dubbed "Fun Friday," and it was always a highlight of the week. We kicked off the day with lively morning huddles, but Fridays had a special magic to them. From fashioning outfits out of bin bags to playing games like "pass the balloon with your lips," the atmosphere was always bursting with energy and laughter. Surprisingly, amidst all the fun, there was also a sense of learning and growth. Looking back, I believe these Friday activities served as a training ground for Laura's future career as a primary school teacher. She found her true calling in this profession, and her passion and expertise have only grown stronger over time. It's hard to believe, but she excels even more now than she did when we worked together.

Working with Laura was an absolute blast. We had so much fun, and it was a time of endless creativity, love, and personal growth. I often look back on those days with fondness, learning valuable lessons along the way. Now, Laura has some natural qualities that create the perfect environment for people to thrive. She's a natural motivator, always pushing us to grow and succeed. She's quick to give praise and feedback, no matter what it is.

During our time together, Laura came up with countless ways to celebrate our team's success. She created incentives and visuals to mark milestones and recognise individual and team **accomplishments**. It made us feel like we were on top of the world. And let me tell you, Laura's **positive** energy and fun-loving nature never wavered. She always encouraged good communication and collaboration. But her biggest strength was the **support** she provided for all of us. It truly made a difference in our lives. She is a true inspiration, and I wish I could bottle her energy. For me, Nurture is all about the energy we give to the change.

Allow me to present the innovative Measurable M.A.P.S Method: a four-step system designed to sustain your momentum and cultivate life-altering habits.

Nurture

Measurable M.A.P.S Method
Motivation - Motivation plays a crucial role in sustaining momentum and cultivating life-altering habits. It's vital that you seek inspiration: Surround yourself with inspiration and motivation. Read books, listen to podcasts, or watch videos that relate to your personal change journey. Find others who have successfully made similar changes, learn from them to provide motivation and valuable insights.
Accomplishment - Accomplishing a habit-related goal or milestone provides a sense of achievement and boosts motivation. When you see progress and experience the satisfaction of reaching a target, it fuels your desire to continue practicing the habit. The feeling of accomplishment reinforces the belief that your efforts are paying off, making you more likely to stick to the habit.
Positivity - Positivity plays a vital role in sustaining personal habits by fostering motivation, resilience, self-belief, mindset shifts, and emotional well-being. Cultivating a positive mindset can significantly contribute to our success in maintaining and sticking to our desired habits.
Support- a support network plays a crucial role in sustaining personal habits by providing accountability, motivation, encouragement, shared experiences, emotional support, collaboration, and feedback. Building and nurturing a support network can significantly increase our chances of successfully maintaining our desired habits over the long term.

Use this Measurable M.A.P.S method to nurture actions from your Positive Performance Plan

1. **What is the inspiring reason for changing this behaviour?**
2. **What quick wins have you accomplished so far?**
3. **What are you grateful for?**
4. **Who can you reach out to for support and encouragement on this behavioural change?**

"Be brave and overcome your busyness. Inspire others to find their own strength to recover. Together, we can make the world a better place."

— LISA POWNEY

7

Wrap up

I hope that you have enjoyed joining me on this journey, we are always working progress so don't stop now. My wish for you is that you have been helped in many ways. Here for me are a few possible reflections:

I hope this book has helped you recognise the trap of busyness that many people fall into. It might have shed light on how busyness can become a default state, leading to stress, burnout, and a lack of fulfilment. This awareness is crucial in breaking free from the cycle of constant busyness and finding a healthier balance in life.

I hope this book may have prompted you to reflect on your priorities and how they align with your busyness. It might have encouraged you to evaluate whether your actions and commitments are aligned with what truly matters to you. This reflection can help you make conscious choices about how you spend your time and energy.

I hope this book has encouraged you to delve into the underlying reasons behind the need for constant busyness. Understanding these root causes can help you address them and make changes that lead to a more balanced and fulfilling life.

I hope this book has emphasized the importance of self-care and taking time for yourself amidst the busyness. It may have encouraged you to prioritise self-care practices that nurture your physical, mental, and emotional well-being. This reflection can lead to implementing self-care routines that support your overall health and resilience.

I hope that completing the exercises in this book has challenged your definition of success and productivity. It might have encouraged you to question society's expectations and find a more authentic and fulfilling definition of success for yourself. This reflection can help you align your actions with your own values and aspirations, rather than external pressures.

I hope this book has inspired you to live more intentionally and mindfully. I hope it has offered strategies for managing time, setting boundaries, and making conscious choices. This reflection can lead to adopting practices that help you live with greater presence and purpose.

Overall, I hope it has prompted deep reflection on how busyness impacts your life and well-being. It has offered insights and strategies for breaking free from the busyness trap and living a more balanced and fulfilling life. It's important to take these reflections and insights and apply them to your daily life, making small changes that lead to a healthier relationship with busyness and a greater sense of well-being.

If it has, then congratulations! You are an amazing individual. You have found the courage to be brave and overcome your busyness. Can you help inspire others?

We are facing a pandemic of busyness, and it is causing unnecessary stress and burnout, affecting our work, our families, and our joy. Together, we can make the world a better place by supporting and uplifting one another. In a world that often feels chaotic and overwhelming, it is essential to prioritise self-care and create space for personal growth. By taking the time to reflect on our own needs and aspirations, we can lead by example and inspire others to do the same.

What can you do?

By sharing our stories of resilience and triumph, we can show others that they too have the strength to overcome their own obstacles. Whether it's through a kind word, a listening ear, or a helping hand, we can make a difference in someone's life by offering support and encouragement. Together, we can create a ripple effect of positivity and empowerment. As we inspire others to find their strength and resilience, they, in turn, can inspire others, creating a chain reaction of personal growth and transformation. By coming together as a community, we can build a support system that lifts each other up and helps us all thrive.

So let us be brave and overcome our busyness, not just for ourselves but for the betterment of the world. Let us inspire others to prioritise their well-being and discover their own inner strength. Together, we can create a world where everyone has the opportunity to flourish and make a positive impact.

If you have enjoyed and found value in what you have read, I'm thrilled to hear that! Taking things to the next level and seeking support to enhance your growth is a wonderful step forward. The Only H.U.M.A.N Bounce-back Recovery Program and Coaching offers a unique opportunity to further develop and cultivate your potential. Accountability plays a crucial role in personal and professional growth, and having a dedicated coach can provide the guidance and support you need to stay on track and achieve your goals.

Through this program, you can expect to receive tailored coaching sessions that focus on your specific needs and aspirations. We will help you identify areas for improvement, set meaningful goals, and hold you accountable for taking action towards your desired outcomes. Remember, personal growth is a continuous journey, and having a supportive network and guidance along the way can make all the difference. If you feel that the Only H.U.M.A.N Bounce-back Recovery Program and Coaching aligns with your aspirations, I encourage you to explore it further and see how it can benefit you.

Wishing you continued success and growth on your journey! You've got this!

About me

The story of my parents is heartbreaking and triggering. They met in 1973 at Rosie's nightclub in Chester, a chance encounter that would change their lives forever. My father, who was working away at the time, and my mother, who lived in Chester, quickly developed a connection. Despite not being together for too long, they decided to embark on a journey together.

My mother came from a small, close-knit family. She was the oldest of two girls and grew up in a modest three-bedroom terrace house. Her mother suffered from multiple sclerosis, and her father, though devoted to her mother, was hard on my mum. Despite the difficulties she faced, my mum had a beautiful and kind soul. She had a way of attracting people and making friends wherever she went. She was a great listener and always made others feel heard. However, she was also a very private person who rarely showed her pain or complained. She carried her burdens silently, keeping her struggles hidden from the world.

When my mum met my father, she was in a vulnerable place. She had recently gone through a divorce after her first husband left her for another woman. My father, on the other hand, came from a small mining village in Wales. He was one of four brothers and faced immense pressure from his older brother and parents to follow in their footsteps and work in the steelworks or the mine. However, my father had different aspirations for his life, which caused tension within his family. Despite the challenges they both faced, my parents decided to take a leap of faith and move to Cardiff together. They rented a flat in the city, starting a new chapter in their lives. However, their relationship was far from perfect. Early on, there were signs of trouble, with small explosions escalating into angry arguments and physical abuse. My mother never shared the details of the first instance of abuse, but she described how my father would apologise and shower her with love and plead for forgiveness afterward.

Less than a year into their relationship, my mother discovered she was pregnant. It was a surprise, as she had been told by doctors that it would be difficult for her to conceive. The news did not improve the situation. In fact, the domestic abuse escalated even further. At this point, my mother had been cut off from her family and friends in Chester, as my father had convinced her to disconnect from them. She had not had enough time to build new friendships or find support in Cardiff.

In February 1974, when my mother was 6.5 months pregnant, a tragic incident occurred that would change everything. My father, stressed and angry, physically attacked my mother in bed. He hit and kicked her out of bed, leaving her in pain and distress. Despite her condition, my mother carried on with her daily chores, including taking the heavy laundry to the laundrette. It was during this time that she started experiencing strong pain and bleeding. Her waters broke, and she went into premature labour with my oldest sister, Sian.

Sian was born weighing only 1lb, with underdeveloped lungs and organs. She was immediately placed in critical care, and my mum was not allowed to hold her due to her fragile state. However, my mum could put her fingers through the holes in the incubator and feel Sian's tiny hand squeezing her finger. Sian fought bravely against all odds, but sadly, after two weeks, she passed away. My parents received the heart-breaking news in the middle of the night, and my mother carried the guilt that my father's abuse may have contributed to the loss of their daughter. She never got the chance to see Sian again, and this haunted her until her last days.

In the months that followed, my father distanced himself from the pain and responsibility. He left my mum to deal with the practicalities, including organising and paying for the funeral. He insisted that she keep it a secret from anyone else. On the day of the funeral, my parents stood alone at the crematorium, watching as a hearse arrived carrying the tiniest white box. The funeral director carried it himself, and as they watched Sian's final journey, no words were exchanged between my parents. My mum, however, thought of Sian every day, her heart breaking for the daughter she could never hold again. I promised my mum that I would find the place where Sian's ashes were scattered and take her there, but we never got the chance to fulfil that promise together. I came into this world just a little over a year later, followed by my two beautiful sisters. My mum carried a heavy burden of anxiety throughout each of her pregnancies, fearing that we had to be girls. My father made it clear that he would reject any boy that was born to him. Looking back now, I realise that his fear stemmed from the belief that he could control girls, but a boy might stand up against him. My mum endured nearly 16 years of staying with him, and the pain she experienced during that time changed her forever, both physically and mentally. The abuse left her with countless physical scars and disabilities, while the trauma she kept hidden ate away at her day by day.

My sisters, like my mum, are an integral part of who I am. We are each a piece of a puzzle, and our shared experiences from childhood have created an unbreakable bond and a deep sense of protection for one another. While we share similarities, as expected, we are also very different. Lorraine, our middle sister, is the most balanced among us. She is tall, beautiful, and intelligent. Lorraine has a practical outlook on life and is incredibly generous. She is a great laugh, and she excels as a mother. Both physically and mentally, she is strong. Unfortunately, our father labelled her as "thick and stupid," a cruel judgment that she has carried with her, always striving to prove herself worthy.

Louise, our youngest sister, is the smartest of us all. She has a natural talent for learning and possesses an amazing ability to connect with people. She is funny and thoughtful, radiating beauty and looks nothing like her age. Our father often teased and punished her on his bad days, leaving her with the same burden of proving herself to someone who saw her as less than she truly is.

As for me, our father labelled me as nothing more than a parrot and a floozy for embracing my femininity. I, too, have carried the weight of his judgment, constantly striving to prove that I am more than what he believed me to be. As children, we witnessed the most horrendous torture inflicted upon our mum. She endured punches, hits, kicks, hair pulling, and food thrown at her. Her clothes and shoes were often ripped off her, and there was often blood and black eyes. Most of these memories were buried deep within our subconscious, only resurfacing in recent times. In the preface, I talked about being haunted with a particular memory after the death of my mum, and I will share this here, in particular. It was a dark winter evening, and my mum was sat on a wooden block next to an open window in the pitch-black dining room, wearing her coat. I hadn't seen her since she set the table for dinner with our father, as she was not allowed to eat with us. I made an excuse to go to the kitchen for a drink, passing through the dining room. My father warned me that if I spoke to my mum, she would get hurt, and we might too. Tears streaming down my face, I whispered to her, "Are you okay?" She nodded, and I quickly got my drink. As I passed back through the room, I mouthed "I love you" before closing the door behind me, locking her away until it was time for her to take us to bed. I hoped she would be allowed to do that tonight. This wasn't a one-off, this happened night after night for years. Even as I write this and think about it again, I am still bewildered by how someone could do such things and get away with it without facing any consequences.

In the weeks and months that followed, I was haunted by memories, beatings of not just my mum but of us girls. The way he would ramp this up when my mum was out. He was a meter reader, which he hated, and he often made us girls stand in the corners of the room with hands on our heads and one of us would be made to wear his rucksack while he told us about how hard his job was and, one by one, would fill it with the heaviest of books. In a particular memory, my youngest sister was wearing this and he threatened that if either my middle sister or I moved, laughed, or cried, she would get more books and we would be hit or have water thrown at us.

In the months that passed, I got angry, I got resentful. How come he got away with this and my mum left this planet unhappy and full of regret? This led me to taking advice from the NSPCC, believe it or not. I was doing some research on adult survivors of domestic abuse and, to be honest, it's very limited, but the NSPCC referred to it and they were really great. They explained to me that I did have the option to report my father to the police still if I wanted to. I didn't have to think about it long. I wanted closure, justice for my mum, and for us girls. The NSPCC started the ball rolling for me, and before long, I was meeting a police officer to report it. I met with my sisters, and for the first time, we talked about our past. We always had an unwritten rule not to go there before then, and between us, we began to remember so much more. The journey of reporting this historical crime was incredibly challenging. Personally, it stirred up a whirlwind of emotions, and I found myself constantly on edge, anxiously waiting for updates from the police. However, the investigation progressed at a painfully slow pace. I was repeatedly told that I was a low priority and that they would do what they could. It took nearly two years before they finally located my father, who had left Wales. They believed they had enough evidence to speak to him provided he was willing to cooperate.

All along, I had hoped for the police to knock on his door and inform him that we had reported him. I wanted him to know that we hadn't forgotten the pain he had caused us before he departed from this earth. After two long years, that moment finally arrived. The police summoned him to the station for an interview, and he complied. However, all he did was deny everything. From an investigative standpoint, that was the end of it. While I initially believed that this was what I wanted, it actually triggered a profound sense of rejection within me. Perhaps deep down, I had yearned for him to admit his wrongdoings, to apologise, and to express regret for not being a father to us. I wanted him to acknowledge the damage he had inflicted upon our lives, stealing our childhood and robbing our real mother of her happiness. Unfortunately, he didn't, and I had to come to terms with that harsh reality. I had to accept it and move forward.

In many ways, I believe I have managed to do so. The patterns I learned in my childhood still linger, but I am more aware of them now. I am actively working on breaking those patterns and healing from the scars of the past.

You may be wondering why I am sharing this deeply personal experience with you. The decision to report my father was driven by a belief that it served a purpose greater than just myself. I held onto the hope that some good would come out of it, not only for me but also for others. I want to raise awareness among fellow adult survivors and offer them support. I want us to learn together, to gain a deeper understanding of the root causes of domestic violence, and to work towards effecting positive change. I realised that it was crucial for me to speak up, even though my confidence had been shaken. It was through the support and guidance of Cheryl and Jane that I was able to rebuild my confidence. Together, they helped me develop a framework that I hope can address one of the underlying causes of domestic violence: burnout and stress.

When individuals experience burnout and stress, their ability to communicate effectively often suffers. They may become more irritable, impatient, and reactive, leading to misunderstandings and conflicts within their relationships. Additionally, burnout and stress can create emotional distance between partners. The overwhelmed individual may withdraw emotionally, becoming less engaged and less available for emotional support. This emotional distance can strain the relationship and create a sense of disconnection. Furthermore, burnout and stress can decrease intimacy and sexual satisfaction. Fatigue and mental exhaustion make it challenging to engage in meaningful physical and emotional intimacy, resulting in a decline in overall closeness.

The influence of burnout and stress on relationships is evident in the escalation of conflict and tension. When individuals are overwhelmed by stress, they become more susceptible to arguments, criticism, and blame. This intensification of conflicts creates a negative cycle that further heightens tensions within the relationship. Furthermore, burnout and stress often result in neglecting self-care and the maintenance of the relationship. People prioritise work and other responsibilities over their own well-being, failing to invest time and effort into nurturing the relationship. This lack of balance and fulfilment can contribute to the deterioration of relationships. Thus, understanding the significance of this issue is crucial.

Throughout my years of coaching and personal experience, I have observed that humans possess an immense capacity to handle challenging situations and cope. However, one area that frequently knocks people off balance is relationships. I have personally felt the profound pain associated with relationship struggles, and it is unlike any other. This has sparked my fascination and desire to explore this topic further. I have always contemplated specialising in coaching individuals in this area, and as I continue to learn and grow, it is a path I will pursue.

Relationships hold a unique position in our lives because they involve deep emotional connections and vulnerability. When a relationship fails, it can deeply impact our well-being and sense of self-worth. Unlike other aspects of life, such as work or hobbies, relationships intricately entwine our lives with another person. The loss of that connection can leave us feeling empty, hurt, and uncertain about our future. Additionally, relationships often involve shared dreams, goals, and plans for the future. When a relationship fails, these hopes and expectations can be shattered, leading to a sense of loss and disappointment. The pain of a failed relationship can be magnified by the investment of time, effort, and emotions that we put into it. Moreover, relationships often involve a significant level of trust and intimacy. When that trust is broken or the intimacy is lost, it can be challenging to recover and move forward. The emotional wounds from a failed relationship take time to heal and may leave lasting scars.

By comprehending the impact of burnout and stress on relationships, we can strive to create healthier dynamics and foster stronger connections. If sharing this knowledge prevents even one family from experiencing the pain that my own family and I have endured, then it will be a worthwhile endeavour. I hope that this book serves as a catalyst for raising awareness about the effects of domestic violence on children, both in the present and into adulthood. Together, let us find ways to understand and address the root causes, and so prevent other families from enduring such suffering.

If this story has impacted you and you would like to message me, please get in touch at *lisa.powney1@gmail.com*

Thank you so much for reading, much love and best wishes to you.

"To my fellow adult survivors of childhood abuse, I want to remind you that you are not alone. You have the power of hope within you, lighting the way towards healing and transformation. Embrace it, nurture it, and let it guide you towards a future filled with hope, strength, and the possibility of a brighter tomorrow."

— **LISA POWNEY**

@lisapowney17

@lisa.twemlow

Lisa (Twemlow) Powney